EDCO
ENGLISH
REVISE WISE

LEAVING CERTIFICATE HIGHER LEVEL

Mary Slattery

Edco
The Educational Company of Ireland

Contents

Revised (beside Introduction section)

Revised (beside Chapter 1 section)

Revised (beside Chapter 2 section)

50 marks (beside Chapter 2)

50 marks (beside Chapter 3)

Revised

Revised

Revised

Revised

Introduction

There are two examination papers in English at Leaving Certificate Higher Level.

Paper 1

Paper 1 is divided into **two sections**. **Both** sections must be answered.

Section I, Comprehending

- The paper will contain **three texts** on a general theme.

- **Two** questions, **A and B**, follow each text.

- You must answer a **Question A** on **one text** and a **Question B** on a **different text**.

- You must **not** answer a Question A and a Question B on the same text.

- Question A generally has three parts. It tests your **understanding** of the given passage and your **response** to it. It carries **50 marks**.

- Question B asks you to write a short piece arising from the content or form of one of the given passages. It is essentially a test of language awareness as used in different settings. It also carries **50 marks**.

Section II, Composing

- You must write on **one** of the titles given – generally seven choices are offered.

- The titles will relate to the general theme of the paper. The quotation taken from the texts will help you focus on the theme of your composition.

- The instructions which follow give you your task, e.g. 'Write an article for a newspaper or magazine'.

- This section carries **100 marks**.

Total marks for Paper 1	Time allotted for Paper 1
200	2 hours 50 minutes

Paper 2

Paper 2 is divided into **three sections.**

- **Section I: The Single Text**

- **Section II: The Comparative Study**

- **Section III: Poetry.**

- You must answer **one question** on the Single Text. **(60 marks)**

- You must answer **one question** on the Comparative Study. **(70 marks)**

- You must answer **two questions** on Poetry – **one question** on the Unseen Poem **(20 marks)** and **one question** on Prescribed Poetry **(50 marks).**

- You **must** answer on Shakespearean Drama, either in the Single Text or as part of the Comparative Study.

Total marks for Paper 2	Time allotted for Paper 2
200	3 hours 20 minutes

How the exam is marked

Every question on the English paper is marked under the following headings:

- **Purpose (P): 30 per cent of marks available for the task.** This is explained by the Department of Education and Science as 'engagement with the set task' – in other words, are you answering the question you have been asked? Does your writing achieve its purpose?

- **Coherence (C): 30 per cent of marks available for the task.** Here you are assessed on the coherence and continuity of the points you are making. Are they linked together in a logical way? Is there a discernible beginning and end?

- **Language (L): 30 per cent of marks available for the task.** Under this heading, you are assessed on aspects of your writing such as vocabulary, use of phrasing and fluency, i.e. your writing style, and how appropriate they are for the task.

- **Mechanics (M): 10 per cent of marks available for the task.** Your levels of accuracy in spelling, grammar and punctuation are what count here. Always leave time to read over what you have written.

Useful websites

- www.skoool.ie

- www.scoilnet.ie

- www.examinations.ie

- www.bbc.co.uk/education

How this book can help you

- Each of the chapters in this book deals with a particular aspect of Higher Level English.

- The chapters are organised according to the order of questions in the examination. You are advised to revise Chapters 1 and 2 together, as there is a close connection between them.

- Each chapter contains information relevant to the topic as well as examination advice and suggested answers.

The study plan

The study plan on p. 116 is there to help you keep track of your revision.

- Work out how much time you have left before the exam and how much time you can devote to each chapter or topic.

- Try to be realistic when setting your targets.

- Tick off the boxes as you meet your goals.

- Re-evaluate your plan if you feel you have been overambitious.

- The night before the exam, check that you have covered all key areas.

How to prepare for English Higher Level

- Be familiar with the features of the different language types: narration, argument, persuasion, information and aesthetic.

- Practise writing in these different language types as regularly as possible.

- Know your texts well for Paper 2.

- For the Single Text, be familiar with aspects such as plot, characterisation and style.

- Learn some key quotations that will illustrate the aspects above.

- Be familiar with the headings for the Comparative Study and what they mean.

- Prepare some key moments from your chosen texts for the Comparative Study.

- Learn some key quotations to illustrate your discussion.

- Know at least five poets for the Poetry section. Do **not** confine yourself to one or two!

- Prepare for questions on each poet by focusing on themes, language and your own response.

- Learn some key quotations to illustrate your points.

- Practise writing exam-style questions in the time you will have in the exam.

- Identify any weaknesses you may have in spelling and grammar and work at eliminating them before the exam.

And remember:

- Reading and writing can be enjoyable experiences. Be confident in your own opinions – don't be afraid to express them.

- Examiners practise positive marking. They want to see what you can do, not penalise you for what you can't.

- Good luck!

1: Comprehending: Part 1

●●●●Learning Objectives

In this chapter you will learn:

- How to recognise and describe the five different forms of language – the language of narration, argument, persuasion and information and the aesthetic use of language.

- How to 'read' a visual text.

Five different forms of language use

- Your study of language for the Leaving Cert involves reading and writing in five different language forms.

- Each of these forms, or **genres**, of language has evolved and flourished because it was considered an efficient way of communicating for a particular purpose.

- These forms of language may overlap in any one text, depending on the needs of the writer.

- If you can learn to identify the basic genre of a piece of writing, you are well on the way to **comprehending** its purpose and **responding appropriately**.

- In the **Composing** part of Paper 1 (Questions B, Section I and Section II), you will then be able to decide which form of language use is most appropriate for the task.

The language of narration

Purpose of the language of narration

- The **purpose** of using the **language of narration**, in speech or in writing, is to **give a connected account of events**, real or imagined.

- Arguably, it is the most common form of language used.

- We are constantly narrating stories of things that happened to us or our friends. For example, we write letters and keep diaries, and we read accounts of other people's experiences in newspaper and magazine articles, in travel writing, or more extended accounts in autobiographies or memoirs.

- Fiction is **imagined narrative**.

Features of narrative writing

- All narrative has a **setting**, i.e. a place and a time.

- It tells what happens or happened in a coherent and logical way, usually chronologically, with a definite beginning, middle and end.

- It **selects specific details** to describe more fully, making use of the following techniques of descriptive writing:

  ❖ Creating vivid images.

  ❖ Appealing to our senses.

  ❖ Using similes and metaphors.

  ❖ Using contrast.

  ❖ Using symbols.

  ❖ Using adjectives and adverbs.

- It contains some comment or reflection. The writer adopts an angle or demonstrates a point of view towards what he or she is saying, even if this is not always stated directly, i.e. the language of narration usually has a definable **tone** (think of **tone of voice** here.)

Top Tip

The choices the writer makes in each of the features above combine to create an impression or evoke an atmosphere to which we as readers respond.

Let's see the features of narrative writing at work in the following example from John McGahern's *Memoir*.

First sentences establish setting, time and place.

When I was three years old, in 1938, I used to walk a lane like these lanes to Lisacarn School with my mother who taught there. We lived with her and our grandmother, our father's mother, in a small bungalow a mile outside the town of Ballinamore.

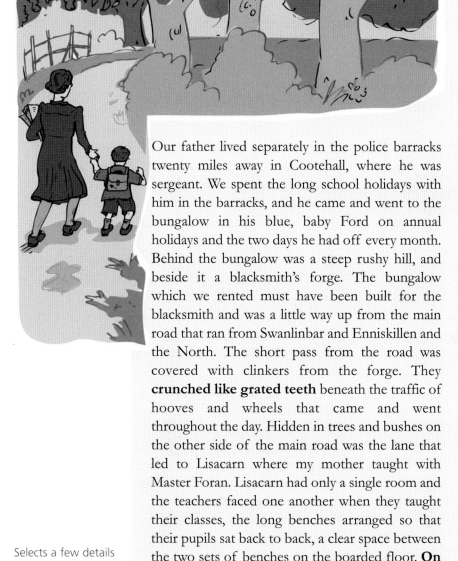

Our father lived separately in the police barracks twenty miles away in Cootehall, where he was sergeant. We spent the long school holidays with him in the barracks, and he came and went to the bungalow in his blue, baby Ford on annual holidays and the two days he had off every month. Behind the bungalow was a steep rushy hill, and beside it a blacksmith's forge. The bungalow which we rented must have been built for the blacksmith and was a little way up from the main road that ran from Swanlinbar and Enniskillen and the North. The short pass from the road was covered with clinkers from the forge. They **crunched like grated teeth** beneath the traffic of hooves and wheels that came and went throughout the day. Hidden in trees and bushes on the other side of the main road was the lane that led to Lisacarn where my mother taught with Master Foran. Lisacarn had only a single room and the teachers faced one another when they taught their classes, the long benches arranged so that their pupils sat back to back, a clear space between the two sets of benches on the boarded floor. **On the window sill glowed the blue Mercator globe, and wild flowers were scattered in jam jars on the sills and all about the room.**

Selects a few details to describe in sensuous images that evoke the atmosphere of the schoolroom.

Note how the writer links the two paragraphs: **Master Foran** has been mentioned earlier. He refers again to the wild flowers in the jam jars and the lane, giving a sense of coherence.

The lane has an obvious importance for him as a place where he was happy. This leads him to reflect on the emotional effect the lane has had on him throughout his life. He further reflects on the strangeness of his experience.

Comments on himself as a child, illustrating with a short anecdote.

Clinkers: furnace slag or cinders; vetches: wild sweet peas; pismires: ants.

Master Foran, whose wife was also a teacher, owned a car, a big Model T Ford, and in wet weather my mother and I waited under trees on the corner of the lane to be carried to the school. In good weather we always walked. There was a drinking pool for horses along the way, gates to houses, and the banks were covered with all kinds of wild flowers and vetches and wild strawberries. My mother named these flowers for me as we walked, and sometimes we stopped and picked them for the jam jars. I must have been extraordinarily happy walking **that lane** to school. There are many such lanes all around where I live, and in certain rare moments over the years, while walking in these lanes, **I have come into an extraordinary sense of security, a deep peace, in which I feel that I can live forever. I suspect it is no more than the actual lane and the lost lane becoming one for a moment in an intensity of feeling, but without the usual attendants of pain and loss.** These moments disappear as suddenly and as inexplicably as they come, and long before they can be recognized and placed.

I don't think I learned anything at school in Lisacarn, though I had a copybook I was proud of. I was too young and spoiled, and spoiled further by the older girls in Lisacarn who competed in mothering me during the school breaks. **I remember the shame and rage when they carried me, kicking and crying, into the empty schoolroom to my mother. Everybody was laughing: I had sat on a nest of pismires on the bank until most of the nest was crawling inside my short trousers.**

Source: John McGahern, *Memoir*

- The question of **purpose** was mentioned earlier. In a memoir, the writer's purpose is clearly to give an account of a certain time of his or her life, which John McGahern does.

- The description of the lane, the schoolroom, the wild flowers – all concrete things that a child remembers – and their link with his mother creates an atmosphere of happiness.

- His reflections on his feelings, first as a child and later as an adult, add to the atmosphere, made even more intense by his realisation that the lane is lost now to him.

- It is possible to say, then, that the **tone** of this passage is both joyful and poignant.

Diary writing

- Diary writing is a type of autobiographical writing that focuses on selected events and reflections.

- The extract below is from a fictional diary, but it shows some of the features of the language of narration as found in diary writing.

Monday, 13 February
9st 1, alcohol units 5, cigarettes 0 (spiritual enrichment removes need to smoke – massive breakthrough), calories 2845.

Events referred to as part of ongoing narrative – to be continued.

Though heartbroken by my parents' distress, I have to admit parallel and shameful feeling of smugness over my new role as carer and, though I say it myself, wise counsellor.

It is so long since I have done anything at all for anyone else that it is a totally new and heady sensation. **This is what has been missing in my life.** I am having fantasies about becoming a Samaritan or Sunday school teacher, making soup for the homeless (or, as my friend Tom suggested, darling mini-bruschettas with pesto sauce), or even retraining as a doctor. Maybe going out with a doctor would be better still, both sexually and spiritually fulfilling. I even began to wonder about putting an ad in the lonely hearts column of the *Lancet*. I could take his messages, tell patients wanting night visits to bugger off, cook him little goat's cheese soufflés, then end up in a foul mood with him when I am sixty, like Mum.

Oh God. Valentine's Day tomorrow. Why? Why? Why is entire world geared to make people

Reflection.

not involved in romance feel stupid when everyone knows romance does not work anyway. Look at royal family. Look at Mum and Dad.

Valentine's Day purely commercial, cynical enterprise, anyway. Matter of supreme indifference to me.

Tuesday, 14 February
9st, alcohol units 2 (romantic Valentine's treat – 2 bottles Becks, on own, huh), cigarettes 12, calories 1545.

Informal, spontaneous language. Elliptical sentences, i.e. words left out. Reveals personality by contradicting herself.

8 a.m. Oooh, goody. Valentine's Day. Wonder if the post has come yet. Maybe there will be a card from Daniel. Or a secret admirer. Or some flowers or heart-shaped chocolates. Quite excited, actually.

Source: Helen Fielding, *Bridget Jones's Diary*

The language of argument

Purpose of the language of argument

● The **purpose** of using the **language of argument**, in speech or writing, is to convince our audience to agree with a particular point of view about a particular topic, supporting it with **reasoned evidence and illustration**.

Features of the language of argument

Argument may make use of one or both of these forms of reasoning:

● Arguing from the **particular to the general**, e.g. the oak trees in the Phoenix Park shed their leaves in winter, therefore all oak trees shed their leaves in winter.

- **Arguing from the general to the particular**, e.g. All cities contain a fair number of homeless people. Dublin is a city. Therefore, Dublin contains a fair number of homeless people.

Each method or argument is effective only if sufficient evidence can be found to support it

- There is a clear **thesis (sometimes called the proposition)** to be discussed. Usually this is a controversial topic.

- The writer adopts a clear position or stance on the matter. However, he or she does not rely on personal opinions to support his/her proposition or thesis.

- The background is usually given, i.e. the need to discuss the matter.

- **Evidence** is produced to support the basic thesis. This may include **illustration, example, statistics.**

- **Counter-arguments (opposing points of view)** may be recognised to give balance, but the writer responds effectively.

- The **tone** is definite and full of conviction.

Coherence and logic are the basis of effective argumentative writing

Common techniques for sustaining a sense of coherence are:

- **Organising effective paragraphs**, i.e. making sure each paragraph has a **topic sentence**. A topic sentence states the main point that will be developed in the paragraph.

- Using **connectors or transitional words** to link paragraphs together.

Connectors

When writing in the language of argument, the following are useful connectors:

- However, nevertheless, but, what's more, furthermore, meanwhile, in addition, in fact, in brief, indeed, all the same, in other words, by the way, on the other hand, as a result, by contrast, of course.

- Paragraphs may also be connected by relating back to a word or idea in the previous paragraph (see examples below).

The language of argument may occasionally overlap with the **language of persuasion**. Both genres have the same aim – to convince others of something. Writing in the language of argument may involve appealing to the reader's emotions as well as reason.

It follows from the above that the **register** (choice of language and voice) of the language of argument is formal.

You will see some of these features at work in the following example from the *Irish Independent*.

Hooked on crime

Strong opening statement makes thesis clear.

Background sketched. Brief illustration given.

Rhetorical question raises issue for reader.

Metaphor is emotive and exaggerated, for sake of effect.

Nobody is immune from violent crime. The last few days have illustrated that vividly. Gang warfare has spilled dramatically over into previously untouched parts of Dublin, and the citizens have reacted with a mixture of alarm and surprise.

But why surprise? No part of the capital – no part of the country, almost – is untouched by the tide of illegal drugs **washing across the island.** Seizures, some of enormous size, are reported daily, but they appear to have little or no effect on the supply. The quantities of cannabis, ecstasy and hard drugs on sale are colossal, and so are the profits.

The traffic has spawned gangs of greater or lesser criminal capacity, but of uniform greed and ruthlessness – and recklessness. They have no difficulty in getting their hands on firearms, which they use with increasing abandon. Inescapably, a turf war or a quarrel within a gang can lead to lethal violence and escalate into the bloody feuds we have witnessed lately.

Links with previous paragraph.

Central argument – crime must be dealt with. Strong, imperative tone of **must**, repeated in following sentences.

Accepts that some progress has been made. Creates sense of balance, which gives further weight to argument.

These events also threaten to involve innocent persons, possibly with fatal results. But this cannot be urged as the prime reason why **the authorities must take swift and effective action.** The feuds are themselves intolerable. No murder is acceptable. The law **must** be obeyed.

Conscious of the public alarm, the Government has made another attempt to bring the streets under control. **It is setting up a special force of 50 experienced Garda detectives under Detective Chief Superintendent Noel White to investigate serious crime.** Their activities, such as surveillance and penetration of criminal plots, can easily be guessed at.

The move is commendable, but the Government need not whinge if it is greeted with more scepticism than similar initiatives in the past. And Ministers should not boast, as they incline to do in this and other areas, about the amount of money spent on it.

Of course they **must** spend whatever it takes. But the criterion by which to judge the initiative is not the amount of money spent. It is the results. And the long-term results are far more important than the short-term gains from a brief, sensational campaign.

Blitz

Sadly, we have been here before. **The murder of Veronica Guerin provoked a blitz which removed some of the worst criminals from circulation for a very long time. Much earlier, the smashing of a major drugs gang by undercover Gardaí seemed – to optimists – to put the problem to rest.** Each time, the optimism was misguided. **The waves receded, only to lash our society again with greater force.**

Optimism is infectious. Not long ago it infected the Minister for Justice, Michael McDowell, who described one crime as the 'last sting of a dying wasp'. These words could haunt him.

The Government **must** face up to something the public know. Violent crime will not be conquered in weeks, or months, probably not in many years.

The Department of Justice and the Garda Síochána **must** steel themselves for a very long campaign. When they win a skirmish, they **must** call it a skirmish. Bulletins prematurely announcing final victory will not be welcome. To come down to cases, the special force now being established **must** remain in existence and **must not** be stood down once the atmosphere calms.

And while one campaign goes on, another should not end. We **need** intelligent and civilised debates on policing and on drugs. We **do not need** bluster and point-scoring. We have had too much of that from the present Government.

Source: Editorial, *Irish Independent*, 17 November 2005

Specific illustrations.

Metaphor continued – creates sense of coherence.

Connecting word.

Repetition of word 'need'.

- You might notice the blend of short and more extended sentences, which gives variety to the style of the passage and makes the argument more effective.

The language of persuasion

Purpose of the language of persuasion

- The **purpose** of speaking or writing in the language of persuasion is to influence others to act or think in a particular way.

Features of the language of persuasion

- As there is an obvious overlap between persuasive writing and argumentative writing, some of the same features may be found. These include:
  - ❖ Use of concrete illustrations/examples.
  - ❖ Some objective evidence given.
  - ❖ Similar language techniques used, e.g. repetition, rhetorical questions.

- However, persuasive writing appeals more to our **feelings** than argumentative writing does.

- Words and images are chosen for their emotional effect rather than their rational or factual qualities. They may appeal to our positive emotions or our negative ones. For this reason, persuasive texts will often use attractive **aural effects**, such as those used in poetry, e.g. **alliteration** and **onomatopoeia**, and **descriptive techniques**, e.g. **visual imagery**, **similes** and **metaphors**.

- **Persuasive language** often has a more **personal** tone than argumentative language.

- Unlike argumentative writing, which is almost always serious in tone, persuasive writing may use humour or irony. **Humour** in particular can be extremely effective. **Wit** or **verbal cleverness** is another effective technique.

- The **language of persuasion** is used in **speeches, religious sermons** and even **informal talks**.

- Because its sole purpose is to **persuade** us to buy a product or project an image or lifestyle for the consumer to admire, **advertising** tends to use the language of persuasion in its most extreme form.

We shall see these features at work in the following examples.

The following extract is from one of the most famous speeches of the twentieth century. It was made by Martin Luther King during the civil rights struggle in the US in the 1960s.

Speaks personally and directly to audience. Introduces notion of **dream**, repeated throughout the speech.

Abstract notion that appeals to feelings of patriotism.

Naming specific place appeals to emotions. Note use of contrast, too.

Repetition.

Emotive, abstract ideas.

Vivid image appeals to emotions.

Biblical language adds to prophetic tone of speech.

I say to you today, my friends, even though we face the difficulties of today and tomorrow, **I still have a dream**. It is a **dream** deeply rooted in the **American dream**. I have a **dream**, that one day this nation will rise up and live out the true meaning of its creed: 'We hold these truths to be self-evident, that all men are created equal.' **I have a dream** that one day, on the red hills of **Georgia**, sons of former **slaves** and the sons of former **slave owners** will be able to sit down together at the table of brotherhood. **I have a dream** that one day even the state of **Mississippi**, a state **sweltering with** the heat of injustice, **sweltering with** the heat of oppression, will be transformed into an oasis of **freedom** and **justice**. **I have a dream** that my four children will one day live in a nation where they will not be judged by the colour of their skin, but by the content of their character.

I have a dream today. I have a dream that one day down in **Alabama** – with its vicious racists, with its governor's lips dripping with the words of interposition and nullification – one day right here in Alabama, **little black boys and black girls will be able to join hands with little white boys and white girls as sisters and brothers.**

I have a dream today. I have a dream that one day every valley shall be exalted and every hill and mountain shall be made low, the rough places will be made straight, **and the glory of the Lord shall be revealed, and all flesh shall see it together.**

Source: Martin Luther King, civil rights speech, Washington, DC, 1963

- It is clear that the **purpose** or **intention** of Martin Luther King's speech is to rouse his listeners to change their attitudes to the question of racial equality. The serious nature of his purpose affects the choice of language he uses.

The next passage illustrates the language of persuasion as used for a less important purpose – to persuade the reader to visit Ireland.

Addresses reader directly. Imperative mood of verbs is strong, convincing.

Note adjectives.

Come and see Ireland's wild side

Ireland's Western region stretches from the hills of Donegal in the North-West to the estuary of the **great** River Shannon in the South. Between, you will find the W.B. Yeats country of Sligo, the **mystic** limestone landscape of the Burren in Clare and the **dramatic** Atlantic coastline of Mayo and Connemara. Add to this the **charming** university city of Galway with its oyster festival and your heart is sure to be captured.

Be part of history

These regions contain most of Ireland's Gaeltacht areas, where the Irish language is still spoken. History is reflected here in its **ancient** sites and monuments such as the Céide Fields in Mayo and King John's Norman castle in Limerick.

The great outdoors

There are also lots of attractions for more sporty people. Horse riding, golf, walking and angling are just a few of the activities available. All water sports, from inland cruising to coastal sailing, and adventure sports are catered for. After all this, you might feel like relaxing with a drink. Well, there's no need to worry on that score, there are lots of **traditional** pubs in the **lively** villages, where the **friendly** locals are sure to make you feel right at home.

Source: Tourism Ireland

- The accumulative force of **adjectives** – *wild, great, mystic, dramatic, charming, ancient, traditional, lively, friendly* – persuade us to see Ireland in a particular light.

- Persuasive texts such as advertisements appeal to the readers' sense of who they are or might be.

- We can **infer** from this advertisement that the reader to be convinced is one who thinks of himself or herself as interested in the scenery, history and literature of Ireland, but who is also active, relaxed and sociable.

- In this way, the text's main technique is one of subtle flattery: these holidays are for well-rounded people.

The language of information

Purpose of the language of information

- The **purpose** of writing or speaking in the language of information is to let the audience/reader know something.

Features of texts written in the language of information

- The content is **factual**: *The train to Galway departs at four o'clock.*

- The **tone** is impersonal and objective. No **point of view** is expressed: *No dogs allowed on beach.*

- The choice of **diction** (words used) is generally neutral. Words are not chosen for their persuasive or emotional effect on the reader.

- Texts written in the language of information are usually organised in a sequential manner, e.g. points are made in chronological order.

- Informative texts may use narration to illustrate their points.

- Instructions, repair manuals, reports of all kinds, memos, agendas and minutes of meetings are examples of texts written in the language of information.

- However, it is not true to say that informative texts will always lack any trace of feeling or attitude, particularly if the purpose is to **entertain** as well as inform. A review, for instance, will contain both information and opinion.

Let's see some of these features at work in the following passage.

The following is an extract from an informative article about the reality television programme *Big Brother*. John de Mol is a Dutch entrepreneur who developed the idea of the show.

Oh, brother…where did it all begin?

Tone is authoritative and impersonal.

Big Brother is nothing short of a phenomenon. Few thought John de Mol's idea would work. Who, after all, would want to watch a group of ordinary people doing ordinary things? Even his fellow executives were **initially** horrified by the prospect of locking people up so their most intimate moments could be spied on by the cameras.

Factual history contains evidence of research.

Yet, de Mol's idea was not entirely new. Among the early prospectors of reality-based television were *Candid Camera* **in 1948,** *The Family* **in 1974, and MTV's** *The Real World* **in 1992.** But de Mol – who had created some of the most popular shows in Holland, including one where ordinary weddings were televised – thought the key to *Big Brother* was to plan it to the smallest detail, to package it in such a way that it would work in any country, for any broadcaster.

But de Mol knew that once he got the show on air in Holland, the rest of Europe, and the world, would topple like dominoes. Peter Bazalgette, the UK television producer who brought the *Big Brother* franchise to the UK, and has traced de Mol's story in a recently published book, *Million Dollar Game*, says the programme works because of our seemingly insatiable diet for voyeurism.

The format that we have become so familiar with **took time to develop.** Intriguingly, de Mol's **initial** plan was to have six people live in a luxury house for one year, but that was abandoned on the grounds that few broadcasters would want to commit to anything for such a long period of time. **Then** he came around to the idea of filming a larger number of people for a far shorter period of time. The most entertaining parts of each day would be edited into a nightly programme, while the internet would show live action from the house.

The programme was initially called *Project X* and *The Golden Cage*, but de Mol **soon** plumped for a more obvious choice – the term memorably coined by George Orwell in *1984*. And de Mol has had to fend off lawsuits from the Orwell estate.

After becoming an instant success when it debuted on Dutch television in 1996, the *Big Brother* format **has become** one of the most popular in television history. The statistics are startling. Viewers across the globe have switched on *Big Brother* more than **18 billion times** and **one billion votes** have been cast for the multinational cast lists.

Big Brother has led the way in television formatting, where a **simple idea and well-devised structure** can be reproduced over and over in all parts of the world. **Together with *Survivor* and *Who Wants to be a Millionaire*, it transformed television as we know it.**

Source: John Meagher, *Irish Independent*, 30 May 2005

Gives facts and figures.

This phrase suggests that the writer's attitude is not merely neutral.

Ends with a summarising statement, doesn't just peter out.

- Some words in **bold** indicate that the information is being conveyed in a chronological order, e.g. *initially*, *soon*, *then*, *after becoming*, *has become*.

- You may also notice that the writer uses **connectors** to give coherence to his piece, e.g. *yet*, *but*.

- The end result is clarity for the reader – an essential feature of the language of information.

Newspaper reports

The main purpose of a newspaper report is to **inform** the reader. A report will attempt to answer the following questions about its topic:

- What.
- Who.
- When.
- Where.
- Why (if known).

Read the following report with these questions in mind.

Irishmen a washout for cleaning, laundry and cooking

A large majority of Irishmen do almost no cleaning, laundry, or cooking at home, a survey by the **Economic and Social Research Institute** has found.

Who carried out survey.

The study, the first of its kind in Ireland, suggests that **81 per cent of men** do no cleaning work on weekdays, while **71 per cent** avoid all cooking or food preparation. The figures 'change little at the weekends', the report adds.

Gives facts and figures.

By contrast, more than two-thirds of all women say they engage in all of these activities on a daily basis. On average, women report spending five hours of each weekday on caring or household work, compared with one hour 40 minutes for men.

But the figures also show that men spend an average of seven hours daily at work or on work-related travel, compared with just three hours 47 minutes for women.

The Irish National Time-Use Survey 2005 was based on a study of 1,000 adults, who filled out diaries – one during the week and one at the weekend – detailing their activities over two 24-hour periods.

What was surveyed, when and where.

A separate survey, also commissioned by the Department of Justice, Equality and Law Reform and compiled by the ESRI, shows that male graduates working in the private sector earn more within three years of graduation than female graduates.

But the advantage is offset by women's lower working hours and their over-representation in the better-paid public sector, so that the overall hourly pay rates are roughly similar for both genders.

The time-use survey suggests that on weekdays, the statistically composite Irish person spends an average of just over eight hours sleeping; four hours in paid employment; one hour 50 minutes on household work; one hour 30 minutes on caring; and five hours on leisure, including a small amount of voluntary or religious activity.

Leisure activity rises to seven hours per day on Saturday and Sunday, but women have 'significantly less leisure time at weekends than men'.

The survey piloted the use of 'light' diary methodology, in which respondents recorded their use of time under 26 pre-defined categories, rather than the 'heavy' diary, which requires a continuous narrative of the respondent's day.

The ESRI said the results provided a 'nationally representative' study and filled an important gap in comparative research.

Source: Frank McNally, *The Irish Times*, 29 November 2005

Final sentence makes general comment on survey.

- The report is written in short paragraphs containing concise, accessible information.

- The writer uses **connectors** to create coherence, e.g. *by contrast*, *but*, repetition of *survey*.

- While the information is given in an unbiased manner, the headline writer has chosen to **interpret** the findings of the survey in a **value judgement**: *Irishmen a washout for cleaning, laundry and cooking.*

The aesthetic use of language

Purpose of the aesthetic use of language

- Unlike the other forms of language we have been discussing, which basically have a functional or practical purpose (to narrate, inform, argue, persuade), the **purpose** of writing in the language of aesthetics is to compose texts that appeal to the reader's sense of beauty or harmony, i.e. to the reader's **artistic sense**. Its primary purpose, then, is to give pleasure.

- Poets, dramatists, screenwriters and **fiction** writers make use of the language of aesthetics.

- As other sections of the exam deal with your response to drama and poetry, as well as film studies, Paper 1 in the exam focuses mainly on the aesthetic use of language as found in fiction.

Features of the aesthetic use of language as found in fiction

- Fiction is **imagined narrative**. It follows that it will use some of the techniques of the language of narration by:
  - ❖ Telling a story.
  - ❖ Creating an atmosphere.
  - ❖ Describing in detail.

But fiction writers extend the techniques of narration and add effects of their own. To create an imaginary world – the world of fiction – the following elements are needed.

The elements of fiction

Plot: The plan, design or pattern of events in a work of fiction

The fiction writer invents a story that he or she then forms into a plot by arranging the events in a way that will arouse the reader's interest. There are usually **four stages** of a plot:

- **Situation or exposition:** Setting is described, characters introduced and their relationships hinted at.
- **Complication:** Tensions or conflicts become more apparent, causing problems for characters.
- **Climax or crisis:** The plot reaches its highest point of tension. This may involve a revelation or surprise that the writer has withheld from the reader, or a moment of physical danger for a character. It is the decisive stage of a narrative that brings about a change of some kind.
- **Resolution:** The final stage of the plot. The lives of the characters usually return to some kind of stability, despite having undergone some changes.

In any work of fiction there may be more than one main plot. A novel may contain a number of plots running simultaneously. Apart from the main plot, there may be connecting **subplots**.

Characterisation

Characterisation is the technique used by the writer to construct a character who may be lifelike and credible but who does not exist in reality.

Characters may be constructed in the following ways:

- **Direct description by the author of appearance or personality:**
    - ❖ 'Fifteen-year-old Jo was very tall, thin, and brown, and reminded one of a colt; for she never seemed to know what to do with her long limbs, which were very much in her way.' (Louisa May Alcott, *Little Women*)
    - ❖ 'She was a woman of mean understanding, little information, and uncertain temper.' (Jane Austen, *Pride and Prejudice*)
- **Indirectly,** when the writer allows them to reveal themselves through **action** and/or **dialogue.**
- How they **interact** with other characters is usually very revealing, too.

In practice, writers will use a combination of these methods to create a credible character.

Point of view

One of the main decisions a writer of fiction must make is: **Who is to tell this story?** In literary terms, this is known as **narrative voice** or **point of view.** It is an important element in characterisation because it will affect the way readers respond to the characters and their actions.

There are **three** main ways of narrating in fiction: first person, third person and omniscient points of view.

1. First person point of view
Here the author uses the first person pronoun, 'I', throughout the novel or story.

The **advantages** of telling a story in this way are that the character comes across as a real person who we can get to know well. He or she can be allowed to speak in an individual, unique way.

The **disadvantages** may be that we are not given access to the other characters' hidden thoughts, so that as readers we share in the narrator's partial understanding of events. Of course, a writer may also use this fact to alert us to the flaws in the narrator's own character.

2. Third person point of view
This is limited to one character or group of characters. Here the author writes in the third person, e.g. 'As they walked home, Elizabeth related to Jane what she had seen pass between the two gentlemen…' (*Pride and Prejudice*), but it becomes clear that the action is being observed from Elizabeth's point of view. We are given access to her thoughts and feelings: 'She grew absolutely

ashamed of herself. Of neither Darcy nor Wickham could she think without feeling that she had been blind, partial, prejudiced, absurd.' (*Pride and Prejudice*)

This is probably the most commonly used method nowadays.

The **advantages** of this method are that it enables the writer to make the reader identify with the main character's situation. It also allows greater flexibility and scope to the writer, who may, in other chapters if it is a novel, change the perspective to that of another character. It is not therefore as one-sided as a first person narrative might be.

The **disadvantage** might be a decrease in intimacy in the **tone** of the novel.

3. The omniscient, or all-knowing, point of view
Here the narrator knows everything about each of the characters, their thoughts and actions, and describes them all with equal detachment.

The **advantage** of this method is that the writer has complete control over what he or she chooses to reveal, as there is no attempt to personalise the point of view that is adopted.

The **disadvantage** may be that the reader will fail to identify sufficiently with the characters.

Setting

- The **setting** of a piece of fiction is the **place and time** in which the characters live and the action takes place.
- We have seen that setting is important in all narratives.
- The writer of fiction, though, usually has an artistic or **aesthetic** purpose in placing the characters and actions in a particular place, time and cultural context. Some of these purposes are:
  - ❖ **To influence the action/plot**: Characters placed on a desert island, for example, will not behave in the same way as those who live in a city.
  - ❖ **To influence the characterisation**: Characters may be affected by their environment, e.g. a background of poverty or wealth may form the basis of a character's personality or motivation.
  - ❖ **To create a specific atmosphere** that will affect the reader's response to the story.
  - ❖ **To hint at themes** that may underlie the story. In this way, setting may be used **symbolically**.

- Some stories seem to arise out of a certain location. Indeed, many novels are named after the places where the events take place, e.g. *Wuthering Heights, Mansfield Park, Animal Farm*.

Themes

- The **theme** of a work of fiction is the **central idea** developed in it.

- A theme is not simply a summary of the storyline. It is a subject which interests the writer and which is discussed in the text or portrayed in it in some way.

- Writers seldom announce their themes directly. A theme is more likely to emerge gradually. Clearly, the theme of a novel will unfold in a more leisurely manner than that of a short story.

- The choices the writer makes in each of the elements of fiction discussed above (plot, characterisation, point of view, setting) will contribute to the reader's recognition of the theme of the story.

Top Tip

Fiction is **narrative** written in the **language of aesthetics**, but it can incorporate other genres of language for fictional ends, so that a novel can contain passages written in the language of **information**, **argument** or **persuasion**. Fiction may 'borrow' the **features** of these genres, making its style rich and complex.

Let's look at the features of fiction at work in two examples, both from novels prescribed as options for the Leaving Cert Higher Level.

> Wuthering Heights is the name of Mr Heathcliff's dwelling, 'Wuthering' being a significant provincial adjective, descriptive of the atmospheric tumult to which its station is exposed in stormy weather. Pure, bracing ventilation they must have up there at all times, indeed; one may guess the power of the north wind blowing over the edge, by the excessive slant of a few stunted firs at the end of the house; and by a range of gaunt thorns all stretching their limbs one way, as if craving alms of the sun. Happily, the architect had foresight to build it strong; the narrow windows are deeply set in the wall, and the corners defended with large, jutting stones.
>
> Before passing the threshold, I paused to admire a quantity of grotesque carvings lavished over the front, and especially about the principal door; above which, among a wilderness of crumbling griffins and shameless little boys, I detected the date '1500', and the name 'Hareton Earnshaw'. I would have made a few comments, and

requested a short history of the place from the surly owner; but his attitude at the door appeared to demand my speedy entrance, or complete departure, and I had no desire to aggravate his impatience previous to inspecting the penetralium.

One step brought us into the family sitting-room, without any introductory lobby or passage; they call it here 'the house' pre-eminently. It includes kitchen and parlour, generally; but I believe at Wuthering Heights the kitchen is forced to retreat altogether into another quarter: at least I distinguished a chatter of tongues, and a clatter of culinary utensils, deep within; and I observed no signs of roasting, boiling, or baking, about the huge fire-place; nor any glitter of copper saucepans and tin cullenders on the walls. One end, indeed, reflected splendidly both light and heat from ranks of immense pewter dishes, interspersed with silver jugs and tankards, towering row after row, on a vast oak dresser, to the very roof. The latter had never been underdrawn: its entire anatomy lay bare to an enquiring eye, except where a frame of wood laden with oatcakes and clusters of legs of beef, mutton, and ham, concealed it. Above the chimney were sundry villainous old guns, and a couple of horse-pistols: and, by way of ornament, three gaudily-painted canisters disposed along its ledge. The floor was of smooth, white stone: the chairs, high-backed, primitive structures, painted green: one or two heavy black ones lurking in the shade. In an arch under the dresser reposed a huge, liver-coloured bitch pointer, surrounded by a swarm of squealing puppies; and other dogs haunted other recesses.

Source: Emily Brontë, *Wuthering Heights*

Aesthetic effects:

- The author's **purpose**, clearly, is to establish the **setting** in which the **characters** will exist and from which the **plot** may evolve. She uses various methods to do this.

Setting:

- The name of Heathcliff's house is also the book's title, which adds to our sense that it will be an important place in the novel.

- Key words suggest the atmosphere of the place: *wuthering* and its explanation, *atmospheric tumult, stormy, power of the north wind, bracing ventilation*.

- The second paragraph indicates that the place has a long history, and indeed introduces one of the key names in the book: Hareton Earnshaw.

- The kitchen and its furniture are described in some detail. The general impression is of size (key words are *immense, towering, vast*). Selected details of the furnishings – the *villainous* guns, the *primitive* chairs and the image of the *huge* dog and the other dogs that *haunted* the recesses – add to our impression that this could be a sinister and even dangerous place to be.

Characters and point of view:

- We are introduced to Heathcliff, one of the main characters of the novel. The reader's curiosity is aroused. Why is he such a *surly owner* of the house? Why is he so indifferent, and even rude, to his guest?

- The story is being told from the perspective of a narrator writing in the first person *I*. The narrator's character is suggested by some small but telling details. He appears curious about the history of the place. He observes it closely (it is his *enquiring eye* that describes the interior of the kitchen). What sort of person might he be?

Plot:

- Earlier on we said that a **plot** usually involves **conflict** of some sort, with **complications** arising from some situation.

- Reading this passage, the reader may speculate what kind of conflict may arise between these two quite different characters.

- Here, the setting plays a role, too, suggesting that the plot may involve strong feelings and perhaps danger.

Top Tip

The choices Emily Brontë has made in her **aesthetic use of language** have combined to create an imaginary world to which we as readers respond.

Dialogue is another technique used by writers of fiction to convey **character**, indicate **setting** and suggest **plot developments**. The following extract from *Pride and Prejudice* is written almost exclusively in dialogue.

'Is Miss Darcy much grown since the spring?' said Miss Bingley; 'will she be as tall as I am?'

'I think she will. She is now about Miss Elizabeth Bennet's height, or rather taller.'

'How I long to see her again! I never met with anybody who delighted me so much. Such a countenance, such manners! And so extremely accomplished for her age! Her performance on the pianoforte is exquisite.'

'It is amazing to me,' said Bingley, 'how young ladies can have patience to be so very accomplished as they all are.'

'All young ladies accomplished! My dear Charles, what do you mean?'

'Yes, all of them, I think. They all paint tables, cover screens, and net purses. I scarcely know anyone who cannot do all this, and I am sure I never heard a young lady spoken of for the first time, without being informed that she was very accomplished.'

'Your list of the common extent of accomplishments,' said Darcy, 'has too much truth. The word is applied to many a woman who deserves it no otherwise than by netting a purse or covering a screen. But I am very far from agreeing with you in your estimation of ladies in general. I cannot boast of knowing more than half-a-dozen, in the whole range of my acquaintance, that are really accomplished.'

'Nor I, I am sure,' said Miss Bingley.

'Then,' observed Elizabeth, 'you must comprehend a great deal in your idea of an accomplished woman.'

'Yes, I do comprehend a great deal in it.'

'Oh! certainly,' cried his faithful assistant, 'no one can be really esteemed accomplished who does not greatly surpass what is usually met with. A woman must have a thorough knowledge of music, singing, drawing, dancing, and the modern languages, to deserve the word; and besides all this, she must possess a certain something in her air and manner of walking, the tone of her voice, her address and expressions, or the word will be but half-deserved.'

'All this she must possess,' added Darcy, 'and to all this she must yet add something more substantial, in the improvement of her mind by extensive reading.'

'I am now no longer surprised at your knowing only six accomplished women. I rather wonder at your knowing any.'

'Are you so severe upon your own sex as to doubt the possibility of all this?'

'I never saw such a woman. I never saw such capacity, and taste, and application, and elegance, as you describe united.'

Source: Jane Austen, *Pride and Prejudice*

- Here the writer allows her characters to reveal themselves by what they say.

- **Charles** comes across as easily impressed, prepared to compliment accomplished young women: 'It is amazing to me…how young ladies can have patience to be so very accomplished as they are.' It is a good-natured remark. But has he really considered the question – what is it to be accomplished? Or does he just take a conventional view? The examples he gives of 'accomplishments' are all of handicraft skills.

- **Darcy** has a more considered attitude to these 'young ladies'. He has higher standards as to what 'accomplished' might mean. Does he reveal himself as hard to please? Maybe he is a little too idealistic. Is there a suggestion of arrogance in his attitude?

- **Elizabeth Bennet**'s reaction to Darcy's views shows her to be more realistic about 'accomplished' young ladies: 'I rather wonder at your knowing any.' She shows here that she is not afraid to speak her mind and is not out to impress him by her views.

- **Miss Bingley**, on the other hand, echoes what Darcy says. Might this suggest a desire to please him? Or perhaps a desire to see Elizabeth contradicted?

Plot – the role of dialogue:

- Even from a short extract such as this, we can glean some information as to how the plot may develop.

- A novel where two of the main characters of opposite sex disagree, and yet appear interested in each other, suggests that the author is writing in the **genre** of **romantic fiction**.

- The plot, then, as we have come to expect in this genre, will be full of complications and obstacles before the happy couple can be united in love.

Setting:

- Even if we didn't know that the extract was from Jane Austen's *Pride and Prejudice*, we could speculate that the setting was upper class (who else had time to sit around discussing 'accomplished young ladies'?).

- The subjects that these characters are interested in places the novel in a certain time, certainly not the modern age.

- The formality of their speech is another indication that they belong to another, more polite, era.

The visual text

Purpose of visual texts

Like written texts, visual texts can be said to have a purpose. And also like written texts, these purposes may be:

- **To narrate:** A visual text is capable of 'telling a story'. Photographs, illustrations and cartoon strips may all have a narrative function.

- **To argue:** Visual texts have proved to be invaluable in making a case for or against something, e.g. the case against war, the fight against crime.

- **To persuade:** Advertising depends to a large extent on effective visuals to persuade the consumer to purchase durable goods or aspire to certain lifestyles.

- **To inform:** The old newspaper cliché that a 'picture is worth a thousand words' applies here. A newspaper report accompanied by a photograph is clearly more informative than one without. Graphs and diagrams present information in a concise way, too.

- **To please aesthetically:** Visual images may have no 'useful' purpose beyond that of making us see the world in a different way or showing us the beauty that surrounds us.

How to 'read' a visual text

When you are asked to 'read' a visual text, you should look at the following aspects.

Content:

- What is the overall image about?

- What details can you see?

Form:

- How is the image composed?

- Is contrast used?

- How are the objects, people, etc. positioned, e.g. in the centre, background, foreground?

- What is the body language, expression, type of clothes of the people in the photographs?

- What features of lighting, colour, camera angle are to be seen?

Context:

- Who are the producers of the text, e.g. advertisers, photojournalists, propagandists?

- Who is the audience for the text? How will they receive it?

Cultural context:

- What cultural understanding and knowledge does the text assume?

- What influences (political, social, religious, etc.) do you think have affected the composition of the text?

Remember that while visual texts may look natural and real, they are constructed by individuals or companies (as in advertising). Choices have been made that affect the way we 'see' the image.

Once you have examined the image carefully with the above aspects in mind, you may begin to **interpret** and **evaluate** the image.

- **Interpretation** involves asking questions about the **purpose** of the text (see above) and the **feelings/responses** it evokes in the viewer.

- **Evaluation** involves forming a judgement about the effectiveness of the text. Does it succeed in what it set out to do? Is it well executed?

If the visual text is part of a group of texts, or accompanies a written text, there are further questions to ask:

- How do the texts relate to each other, e.g. do they **complement** or **contrast with** other texts?

- What overall impression is created by the texts as a group?

- How do the visual texts relate to the written text?

Let's look at some of these aspects of visual texts as they relate to the following example.

The visual images are taken from an exhibition of photographs, entitled *The Family of Man*, which was first shown in the Museum of Modern Art, New York in 1955.

Photographs by Edward Steichen reprinted with permission of Joanna T. Steichen

Analysing the visual text

Content

The title of the exhibition indicates the **purpose** and **general content** of the photographs. *The Family of Man* suggests a desire to **inform** an audience of the diversity of human experience. It also indicates an intention to **celebrate** this diversity, and to **persuade** an audience to appreciate it.

- The planet earth at the centre of the text causes us to focus on the idea of unity in the world – that all people are part of this human family.

- Each photograph shows a different aspect of human life. But the content of each photograph cannot be seen in isolation, as it forms part of a collection with a collective title.

- The photographs are representative of the human family, showing men, women and children.

- We see people in **contrasting** situations: work and play (no. 2, 3, 4, 10), rural and urban (no. 2, 6, 7, 10) and different ethnic groups (no. 1 and 6 show non-Western people).

- We also see people at different stages in their lives: young and old (no. 4) and middle-aged (no. 3, 5).

- The photographs record people at important moments: marriage (no. 7), experiences of parenthood (no. 6, 8, 9), grief or trauma (no. 5).

- Other **contrasts** in content show diversity of experience: happiness (no. 2, 3) and sadness (no. 5).

Form

- As the content seeks to show the variety of human experience, the form of the photographs naturally differs, too.

- The photographer has used **close-up camera angles** in no. 1, 5, 8, 9. The people in these photographs dominate the centre of the **frame**. The effect is to convey the **mood** of the photographs in an immediate way, from joy (no. 1, 8, 9) to sorrow (no. 5).

- In contrast, the photographer uses a high angle shot in no. 7. This has the effect of capturing the communal nature of the celebration of marriage. A medium shot of the two people, each equally balanced, in no. 4, suggests the dual nature of the relationship.

Context/cultural context

- The photographers who produced these texts were clearly working in the public sphere – these are not photographs of a 'family' for private consideration.

- The variety of the photographs would ensure that there is something in them for everybody.

- We cannot ignore the date of the exhibition – 1955, only 10 years after the end of World War II. Might this have influenced the purpose of the exhibition – to help heal the divisions caused by the war, by showing that we are all part of the 'family of man'?

Key Points

Note: In Chapter 2 you will see how these points can be applied to exam questions.

- Language may be studied under five **different genres (types)**: narration, argument, persuasion, information and the language of aesthetics.

- These forms may overlap in any one text.

- The **language of narration** gives a connected account of events. It involves **narrating**, **describing** and **reflecting**.

- Texts written in the language of narration include **autobiography**, **biography**, **letters**, **diaries** and **travel writing**.

- The **language of argument** makes a case in favour of, or against, a controversial topic. It involves **reasoning**, **supported by evidence**.

- It occasionally overlaps with the **language of persuasion**.

- The **language of persuasion** convinces the reader to accept a point of view or to purchase a product. It involves **appeals to the emotions**.

- Texts written in the language of persuasion include **speeches** and **advertising**.

- The **language of information** informs the reader about a situation or process. It involves using **objective language** and **facts**.

- Texts written in the language of information include **reports**, **memos** and **instruction manuals**.

- The **aesthetic use of language** involves language used primarily for artistic purposes – it has no 'useful' purpose. It includes **fiction**, **poetry**, **drama** and **screenwriting**.

- **Fiction writing** involves **setting**, **plot**, **characterisation**, **dialogue** and **theme**.

- Writers and authors of visual texts **choose techniques to create a particular response**.

- Reading a **visual text** involves examining its **content**, **form** and **context**.

2: Comprehending: Part II

● ● ● **Learning Objectives**

In this chapter you will learn:

- How to apply your study of language forms in comprehending texts.

- How to answer comprehension questions in the exam.

Introduction

Comprehending any text is like having a conversation with the author. Above all, writers want to communicate with their readers.

As in any meaningful conversation, comprehending involves understanding the writer's ideas (**what** he or she is saying), responding to what the writer says and evaluation.

Understanding the writer's ideas

Questions that look for an understanding of the writer's ideas are usually found **near the beginning** of a series of questions. They may be phrased in different ways:

- What, according to the writer, is the main problem/advantage/etc.?

- What information about…did this passage give us?

- What are the main points made by the writer of this passage?

These kinds of questions require you to **summarise** the writer's ideas. **Use your own words** as far as is reasonably possible and **do not** introduce ideas of your own at this stage. Other questions should give you an opportunity to do so.

Understanding what the writer says also involves **why** he or she is saying it, i.e. the writer's **intention** or **purpose**.

Responding to what the writer says

Questions seeking a response may be phrased in different ways:

- To what extent would you agree with…?

- What impact did this visual image/piece of writing have on you?

- Did this passage appeal to you?

These kinds of questions require you to **give your own views**, but they **must be based** on what the writer has said, i.e. you should focus clearly on the passage itself and either **support** or **refute** the text with extended points or illustrations from your own experience.

Evaluation

You may be asked to **evaluate** or **assess the success** of a particular piece of writing or a particular visual text. These kinds of questions may be phrased in different ways:

- Did the writer succeed in convincing you that…?

- Do you think that the written and visual elements of the text go well together?

- Is this a good piece of writing, in your view?

These kinds of questions require you to focus on the **techniques** used. You should discuss them in some detail, giving examples, and respond accordingly.

Your study of the different forms of language (see Chapter 1) should certainly help you in answering these types of questions.

Remember, within any one text there can be a mixture of language forms. However, the most important question to ask yourself is: What is the chief purpose of this piece of writing? Is it:

- Telling a story? (narration)

- Arguing for or against something? (argument)

- Persuading us to think in a certain way? (persuasion)

- Letting us know something? (information)

- Telling a story, with characters and a possible plot? (aesthetic use of language)

Examination section

The **Comprehending Section** of **Paper 1** contains **three texts** on a specific theme, as stated on **page 1**, the instruction page of the paper.

Before you begin:

- Make sure you note the **theme** of the paper.

- Themes that have been given since the examination began in 2001 are: **Irishness (2001), Family (2002), Journeys (2003), Work and Play (2004), Ordinary Lives (2005), Pretence (2006).**

- Everything on the paper relates to the given theme, so think of the texts as a help or resource.

- Remember, **one** of the texts will be a **visual text**, which may be accompanied by a short written text.

- Each of the other two texts will also be accompanied by a small visual cue which can help you to place it in context.

- Read **each** of the texts **before** you start to answer any questions.

Next, focus more closely:

- Be careful to note the **title** of each of the texts. Questions sometimes focus on the appropriateness of the title.

- Glance at the accompanying visual.

- **Read** the brief introduction to the passage at the top of the page. This is **vital**, as it will give you crucial information as to the possible **language genre** it belongs to.

- Take note of the **number of questions** you are required to answer. (To date, **three** questions have been set on each passage.)

- **Note:** At this stage it is important to look at the choices offered in **Question B** that follows each text. **Question B** is the functional writing task that arises from the context, content or form of the text in **Question A.** You may **not** answer a Question A and a Question B on the same text.

- Therefore, if one of the functional writing tasks set in Question B appeals to you rather than the others, direct your attention to one of the other texts for Question A.

Having made your choice:

- Read the passage carefully.

- Look at the questions before reading it again.

- This time, keep in mind the context in which it was written (an extract from a novel? a newspaper feature?) and any features of style that you may notice.

- Begin your answers.

- You are not required to write at any specific length, but bear in mind that your answer should deal as fully as possible with the question.

Total marks for Comprehending, Paper 1, Question A	Time suggested
50	35 minutes

Sample questions and answers

Text 1, Leaving Cert 2005

General theme: Ordinary Lives

Top Tip

You will note that the passage is taken from a memoir, which should prepare you for encountering some of the features of the language of narration.

Margaret Foster writes about her grandmother, Margaret Ann Hind, a domestic servant in Carlisle, a town in the north of England, in the 1890s. Her book is called Hidden Lives – A Family Memoir.

Top Tip

Remember that titles are important – they can direct our reading of a text or make us aware of another way of interpreting it.

An Ordinary Life

The life of Margaret Ann, my grandmother, was narrow. The physical hardship, the sheer energy and strength needed to get through each day, was commonplace. She *expected* to be down on her knees scrubbing, up to her elbows in boiling or freezing water, washing and rinsing dishes, rocking on her feet with weariness after hours of running up and down stairs. When she reminisced in later life, it was always without any trace of resentment. Her expectations were low. She was expected to carry on as she was until she dropped. Or married.

Marriage was always an option. Marriage was possibly, but not definitely, or even probably, an escape from servitude. If she married, she knew she'd still have to cook and clean and wash and mend, and without the help of the kind of servant she was to the Stephensons unless she married a rich man. The chances of this happening were nil. Who, in Carlisle, among the servant class, married rich men? Rich, eligible men were few and far between, and girls like Annie Stephenson from good families ever on the lookout for them. But there was rich and rich after all. Plenty of tradesmen around who did quite well for themselves, would could afford to rent or even to buy decent houses and to lead comfortable enough lives. The market was full of them. Plenty of money there, especially among the butchers, with Carlisle being such a big meat-eating place. On Saturday afternoons Margaret Ann would go to the market to buy the meat for Sunday. She went through the glass doors and down the little cobbled hill where the butchers' stalls now were. Some butchers had more than one stall. They had three or four together, positive empires. The meat hung from the ceiling on hooks, whole carcasses of pig and lamb and beef, and on the tiled counters below lay the cut-up portions; the bright red stewing steak, the dark slabs of liver, the great coils of pale, putty-coloured sausage, the crimson rounds of mince, the stiff row of chops.

Thomas Hind was proprietor of stall number 4. This stall was clean. The carcasses didn't drip blood, the meat on the counter did not lie in puddles of it, the bin for fat wasn't nauseatingly visible. The floor always seemed freshly sawdusted, the aprons of the assistants were spotless. Even though his prices were not the cheapest, there was always a queue at Thomas Hind's. Margaret was a patient queuer. She never attempted to push herself forward but waited her turn calmly. She engaged in none of the banter that other customers seemed to like. She stated her requirement and that was that beyond a please and thank you. These were exactly the qualities which aroused Thomas Hind's interest. He noticed her precisely because of her curious quality of stillness. In 1893, when she first began buying meat from him, he was thirty-five years old and unmarried. His father had been a butcher and so had his grandfather, and as the only son he was always expected to take over the family business. His father had died when Thomas was a child and his mother, Jane, had become a butcher herself in order to keep the business going for Thomas to inherit. His debt to her was strong and he acknowledged it by now supporting not just her but two

of his three sisters (the third had married). He was prosperous enough for them to marry. He was notoriously hard to satisfy and was teased about his high standards by his sisters who despaired of him ever approving of any girl. For four years he observed Margaret Ann quite contentedly, and then, when his mother died in 1897, decided the time had come for him to court her very seriously. Nothing impetuous about Tom.

So it was a slow affair, this courtship, three years of best boned and rolled sirloin, shoulder of lamb, leg of pork, three years of pounds of sausage, best back bacon, ham on the bone. A lot of meat, a lot of pleasantries, a lot of cap-doffing on Tom's part and head-inclining on Margaret Ann's. One Saturday, towards the end of the afternoon, when there were no assistants to hear and smirk, no customer other than Margaret Ann to hear and speculate, he asked her if she would care to go with him and his sisters out to the Burgh marsh for a breath of sea air. He was very much afraid she would refuse, even be offended, but no, she smiled and said she knew his sisters from church and would be glad to accompany them if she could get time off.

Source: Margaret Foster, *Hidden Lives*

Question A

(i) Write a paragraph in which you comment on the appropriateness of the title of this text, 'An Ordinary Life'. (15)

(ii) What impressions of the characters of Thomas Hind and Margaret Ann do you get from this passage? Give reasons for your answer. (15)

(iii) Did the description of the market bring it to life for you as a reader? Support your answer by reference to the text. (20)

Sample answer for (i)

In my opinion, the title **'An Ordinary Life'** is appropriate for this text. The two main characters are ordinary, hard-working people. Margaret Ann's job as a servant to a rich family was one which many working-class people had in the 1890s. The work she did, the writer tells us, was **commonplace**. There is no suggestion in the text that she was unhappy – in fact, the writer comments that **her expectations were low**. Thomas Hind's position as a tradesman, a butcher, meant that he would have been able to live a life of relative comfort, but his expectations would probably have been just as modest as Margaret Ann's.

> **Top Tip**
>
> Remember how a narrative writer creates character – by describing what they do, say, how they see the world and how others react to them. Although there is no dialogue in the passage, the writer gives us quite a full picture of the two characters.

The story of their courtship suggests that they were an ordinary couple who wanted some happiness in life, but circumstances, as well as their cautious natures, caused them to wait for the right moment before commencing their life together. If we remember that the memoir is set in the last part of the nineteenth century, the title is appropriate for the context and for the experiences of the two main characters.

Sample answer for (ii)

My impression of **Thomas Hind** is that he was a hard-working man with a great sense of duty. He kept his butcher's stall meticulously clean, and it seems to me that he also had high standards in his personal relationships. He recognised that his mother had worked hard to pass on the business to him and he repaid his **debt to her** willingly, supporting her and two of his sisters without putting his own happiness first. He obviously noticed Margaret Ann early on but waited for four years, until his mother was dead, to court her. This suggests that he was a patient man – indeed, the narrator makes the comment that there was **'nothing impetuous about Tom'**.

However, my impression is also that he was a little too cautious in his behaviour. He waits until all the other customers have gone to ask Margaret Ann to go out with him. He seems to fear that people might **smirk** or **speculate** about his private life, which suggests to me that he is a little too suspicious of other people. He is also afraid of being rejected, so I got the impression of a shy, sensitive man.

Margaret Ann comes across as equally hard-working, as described in the first paragraph. The narrator hints that she was on the lookout for a man to marry,

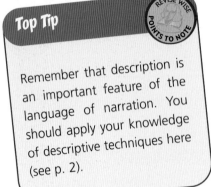

Top Tip

REVISE WISE POINTS TO NOTE

Remember that description is an important feature of the language of narration. You should apply your knowledge of descriptive techniques here (see p. 2).

having considered it as an option to escape from her life as a servant. My impression is that she would have had high standards for a potential husband, as Thomas did for a wife, and that she would deliberately wait for someone who seemed to meet these standards. We see his butcher's stall from her point of view, clean and well-kept. Her behaviour in the queue gives the impression of a polite, reserved person. These traits suggest that she would have approved of his sense of privacy, not asking her out in front of other people. The main impression of her character I get from the passage is that, like Thomas, she was a patient, cautious person. In fact, I feel that they are both very suitable partners for one another.

Sample answer for (iii)

The writer's descriptive techniques certainly brought the market to life for me. Images of the carcasses hanging on hooks above the tiled counters remind me of the butchers' shops of the past. The adjectives she uses to describe the meat are particularly vivid: the **bright red** stewing steak, the **crimson** mince, with the contrasting **dark slabs** of liver and **pale, putty-coloured** sausage. She makes us see the shapes of the different types of meat, some of it cut into **slabs**, lying in **coils**, piled high in **mounds** or placed in **stiff rows**. These images appeal to our sense of sight, but also to our sense of touch, which she continues into the next paragraph when she mentions the carcasses that would **drip blood** or **lie in puddles** of it. The word **nauseatingly**, referring to the bin for fat, effectively brings the market to life, for me, as a rather unpleasant place to be. No wonder, then, that Thomas Hind's stall, which is described in contrasting images of cleanliness, was attractive to Margaret Ann.

The other aspect of the market that brought it to life for me was the description of the customers, some engaging in banter with the butchers, others, like Margaret Ann, politely asking for what she needed and leaving it at that. This, and the fact that Thomas and Margaret's courtship began there, makes it seem a more human kind of place.

Text 2, Leaving Cert 2005

Visual text: Ordinary Lives in War Time

The following text consists of a written and visual element. The written text is adapted from an introduction by documentary photographer Jenny Matthews to her book of photographs, entitled **Women and War**.

Mozambique 1986. Soldier with his baby son just before he returns to the front next morning.

El Salvador 1986. An afternoon dance.

Bosnia 1994. Twenty-year-old Spanish soldier serving with UN waving Red Cross convoy over narrow bridge.

Eritrea 1988. Fighter back at base after battle.

Introduction by Jenny Matthews

From the beginning I was interested in covering foreign stories – starting with Central America in the early eighties, a bit off the map for the British media but an exciting place with revolutionary groups fighting guerrilla wars in the mountains.

One visit led to another and I learned about war. Although I have often worked where pictures in the news were of the front line confrontation, I was more interested in what was going on behind the scenes, and that usually involved looking at how women were holding everything together. Some of the wars that I've tiptoed around have been major international conflicts – the Balkans, Middle East, Rwanda, Afghanistan – but others have been practically invisible.

I have not been everywhere and this is not a complete record of world conflict; it is my take on recent history, recognising the lives of remarkable women, ordinary people surviving as best they can. As I've travelled I've kept diaries, and the notes from these accompany the photos. All my work has been done in co-operation with a network of people, journalists, friends, fixers, drivers, translators, development workers. Without them it would be hard even to leave home. It has been a great privilege for me to be a photographer, to wander into other people's lives, often uninvited, but usually made embarrassingly welcome. I have lurked around some nasty corners of the world and come across the raw edges of life and death; an infinity of sorrow and fear, but more often than not, tempered with the hope that things will be better for the next generation.

Source: Jenny Matthews, *Women and War*

Question A

(i) Which of the four images makes the strongest impact on you? Give a reason for your answer. (15)

(ii) Do you think that the introduction to the collection of images is an interesting portrayal of Jenny's life as a news photographer? Give reasons for your answer. (15)

(iii) 'I learned about war…[but] I was more interested in what was going on behind the scenes.' From your reading of the introduction and the photographs, what impression do you have of how people's lives are touched by war? (20)

Sample answer to (i)

The photograph that made the strongest impact on me was number 1, the picture of the soldier in Mozambique. The close-up of the soldier holding his baby son is a moving indictment of the cruelty of war, especially if we remember that war destroys families like this.

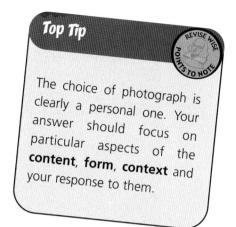

Top Tip

REVISE WISE POINTS TO NOTE

The choice of photograph is clearly a personal one. Your answer should focus on particular aspects of the **content, form, context** and your response to them.

The contrast between the strong father, whose frame fills the picture, and the small child in his arms makes me think of the joy of parenthood. The expression on the father's face, the tender way he holds his child, seems to me to symbolise the great bond between parents and children. But the photograph also makes me aware of the fragility of this relationship, when you consider that this moment of closeness could possibly be the last they will ever have. We realise this because of the caption underneath the image, which places it in context for us: Mozambique 1986, taken just before the soldier has to return to the front. The fact that he is a soldier who will have to kill other people's sons or fathers in war in the future further underlines the poignancy of the image.

For these reasons, the image made a strong emotional impact on me.

Sample answer to (ii)

Yes, I find her description of life as a news photographer fascinating, as she seems so enthusiastic about it herself. She refers to Central America, where she first recorded war stories, as an 'exciting' place, though it was obviously dangerous, too, with guerrilla warfare in the mountains. She has been present at a number of different conflicts, both major and minor. Not only has she photographed the action on the front line, she has also covered the events behind the scenes, taking particular interest in the experiences of women in wartime.

I was impressed by and interested in her attitude to her career, too. Nowhere does she come across as cynical or exploitative. In fact, she sees herself as having been 'privileged' to be a news photographer, encountering 'remarkable women' and friendly people. It is clear that she sees herself as working as part of a team, with journalists, translators, etc., and this is an interesting aspect of the job.

In the final sentences, she succeeds in conveying how seriously she views her career. Her language becomes more sombre. She refers to her experience of 'life and death', 'sorrow and fear' and finishes with an expression of 'hope' for the future.

In my view, her portrayal of her life gives us a fascinating insight into the adventure, variety and significance of the career of a news photographer.

Sample answer to (iii)

Both the introduction and the photographs give me the impression that war is a catastrophic event for most people. Matthews speaks of how she felt some women in wartime were 'holding everything together'. She uses emotive phrases like 'the raw edges of life and death' and 'an infinity of sorrow and fear', which suggest that the experience of war is utterly traumatic. Her photograph of the soldier and his baby son adds to my sense of the sorrow of war, when we consider that the father may not live to see his son grow up. Photograph number 3, showing a twenty-year-old Spanish soldier, reinforces the impression of how war involves young people, sadly, in situations of conflict and danger. The fourth photograph, of a woman soldier in Eritrea, also suggests that modern warfare in particular affects men and women alike.

But the introduction and the photographs give me another perspective on war, too. Matthews mentions her satisfaction at being able to take photographs and the co-operation she found from others. It is as if the experience of war can bring out the best in people. It can even be exciting. In my view, the photographs contribute to this idea. The expressions on the faces of the young Spanish soldier and the woman fighter do not seem frightened or miserable. Both pose for the camera as if they are somehow proud of their roles. In fact, the young woman in photograph number 4 looks almost happy, standing casually with her weapon slung over her shoulder, as if in a fashion shoot.

Top Tip

You will notice that the answer to this question is longer than the others. Answers worth 20 marks should, generally speaking, be longer than those worth 15.

Photograph number 2 suggests a further aspect to how people live their lives in wartime. The soldier takes the opportunity to dance in the afternoon, presumably during a lull in the fighting. To me this gives the impression that many people do not allow war to destroy their joy in ordinary human activities – just as the woman fighter in photo number 4 seems to be interested, despite everything, in her clothes and personal appearance. These photographs bear out the writer's words that people's sorrow in wartime can still be 'tempered with hope that things will be better'.

Practice question

Comprehension passage, Leaving Cert 2002

Text 3, Families in a Time of Crisis

This text is an extract from the novel The Grapes of Wrath *by the American writer John Steinbeck. The novel tells the story of poor farming families who are forced to travel hundreds of miles across America in search of a living. In this extract we learn how the desire of families to support one another leads to the setting up of a society in itself. The novel was first published in 1939.*

The cars of the migrant people crawled out of the side roads on to the great cross-country highway, and they took the migrant way to the West. In the daylight they scuttled like bugs to the westward; and as the dark caught them, they clustered like bugs near to shelter and water. And because they were lonely and perplexed, because they had all come from a place of sadness and worry and defeat, and because they were all going to a new mysterious place, they huddled together; they talked together; they shared their lives, their food, and the things they hoped for in the new country. Thus it might be that one family camped near a spring, and another camped for the spring and for company, and a third because two families had pioneered the place and found it good. And when the sun went down, perhaps twenty families and twenty cars were there.

In the evening a strange thing happened: the twenty families became one family, the children were the children of all. The loss of home became one loss, and the golden time in the West was one dream. And it might be that a sick child threw despair into the hearts of twenty families, of a hundred people; that a birth there in a tent kept a hundred people quiet and awestruck through the night and filled a hundred people with the birth-joy in the morning. A family which the night before had been lost and fearful might search its goods to find a present for the new baby. In the evening, sitting about the fires, the twenty were one. They grew to the units of the camps, units of the evenings, and the nights. A guitar unwrapped from a blanket and tuned – and the songs, which were all of people, were sung in the nights. Every night relationships that make a world,

established; and every morning the world torn down like a circus. At first the families were timid in the building and tumbling worlds, but gradually the technique of building worlds became their technique. Then leaders emerged, then laws were made, then codes came into being. And as the worlds moved westward they were more complete and better furnished, for their builders were more experienced in building them.

The families learned what rights must be observed – the right of privacy in the tent; the right to keep the past hidden in the heart; the right to talk and to listen; the right to refuse help or to accept, to offer or to decline it; the right of son to court daughter and daughter to be courted; the right of the hungry to be fed; the rights of the pregnant and the sick to transcend all other rights. And as the worlds moved westwards, the rights became rules, became laws, although no one told the families. And with the laws, the punishments – and there were only two – a quick and murderous fight, or ostracism; and ostracism was the worst. For if one broke the law his name and face went with him, and he had no place in any world, no matter where created.

There grew up a government in the worlds, with leaders, with elders. A man who was wise found that his wisdom was needed in every camp, and a kind of insurance developed in these nights. A man with food fed a hungry man, and thus insured himself against hunger. And when a baby died a pile of silver coins grew at the door flap of the tent, for a baby must be well buried, since it has had nothing else of life.

Source: John Steinbeck, *The Grapes of Wrath*,
Penguin 20th Century Classics, 1992

Question A

(i) How does the language of the opening paragraph suggest the powerlessness of the migrant people? Support your answer by reference to the text. (20)

(ii) In the remainder of the passage, how does Steinbeck show the bonds between people becoming stronger and more powerful? Support your points by reference to the text. (20)

(iii) "There grew up a government in the worlds…' Look again at the final paragraph. What, in your view, is the most important thing it says about people? Explain your answer, illustrating briefly from the text. (10)

Key Points

- An awareness of a writer's **purpose** is helpful in **comprehending**.

- **Comprehending** involves understanding **what** is written and **how** it is written, i.e. the writer's style and techniques.

- It also involves **responding** and **evaluating**.

- **Section 1** of **Paper 1**, **Question A** contains **three texts**, one of which is generally a **visual text**.

- The visual text may also be accompanied by a written text.

- The texts will all relate to a particular **theme**. **Note this** carefully.

- Read **all** of the texts before you choose to answer one of them.

- Read each **Question B (Functional Writing Task)** before you answer Question A, as you will not be able to answer A and B on the same text.

- There are generally **three questions** to be answered on the chosen text.

- Note **marks allotted** to each question. Answers awarded 20 marks should be more detailed than those worth 15.

- Suggested time for Comprehending, Question A: **35 minutes**.

- **Total marks**: 50.

3: Comprehending: Paper 1, Question B

●●●**Learning Objectives**

In this chapter you will learn:

● How to apply your understanding of language forms in answering Question B, Section I, Paper 1.

Introduction

In Question B in the comprehension section, you will be asked to show your understanding of how language works in different situations. You will have to write a short piece based on the text you have just read.

This is essentially a **functional writing task** in that the context, content and form will be set within the question.

This does not mean that you cannot be creative, but it does mean that you should follow the conventions or standard ways of writing as required.

The table on the next page lists some possible tasks for Question B and the range of language categories they may involve.

Top Tip

Question B may test your language awareness in any of the five main genres, so be prepared!

●●●	Narration	Argument	Persuasion	Information	Aesthetic use of language
Letter (LC 2002, 2003, 2004, 2005, 2006)	X	X	X	X	
Speech/talk (LC 2001, 2002, 2003, 2004)	X	X	X	X	
Instructions/ guidelines (LC sample paper, 2000)				X	
Advertisement/ brochure (LC sample paper 2000, 2002)			X	X	X
Diary entries (LC 2001, 2003, 2005, 2006)	X				X
Review	X	X		X	
Description	X				X
Report (LC 2006)				X	
Memos/ proposals (LC 2005)		X		X	
Obituary	X			X	

How to approach the functional writing task

You will need to take the following into account:

● **Purpose:** What is the chief purpose of the piece of writing – to inform, argue, persuade, etc.? Remember the five **language genres** here.

● **Audience:** Who will receive the letter, listen to the talk, read the report, etc.? If written for a newspaper or magazine, what sort of readership is involved?

Top Tip

Even an informal context may be bound by its own rules. To write a note to a milkman ordering two pints of milk in a formal way is as inefficient a use of language as to write a letter to the school principal as if she were your best friend.

- **Context**: Where and when is the piece of writing taking place? Is it a public or private situation, e.g. a speech or a diary entry? Does the text on which it is based suggest a particular context, a time and/or place?

- **Register**: The language you use – the tone, vocabulary, etc. – should reflect the **purpose** of the task. As we saw in Chapter 1, each genre of language has its own features and characteristics. Choice of register will be greatly influenced by the **audience** for the task. In ordinary life, everyone has a repertoire of different styles of language they use in different contexts. This section of the paper tests your awareness of appropriate language use.

- **Form**: This will depend on the requirements of the task, its purpose and audience. The idea of 'form' is associated with the idea of rules and conventions and of following established ways of writing. It also suggests the 'shape' or 'structure' of a piece of writing.

Example 1: Write a letter to the editor on a subject that concerns young people

Dear Sir,

I would like to take issue with your correspondent's view that the points system in the Leaving Certificate is democratic and fair. Surely democracy is about choice. For two years now I have suffered the stress of preparing for the examination. I have never thought that I have had any choice but to do so. Where is the democracy in this?

Other countries, such as the United States, have devised ways of admitting students into college without imposing two years of misery upon their young people. A standardised aptitude test would offer anonymity and a level playing field as much as the Leaving Cert does without imposing a rigidly competitive curriculum on students. Schools might then be able to devise a more flexible curriculum to include subjects such as political affairs, relationship education and even driving lessons.

If we want to teach young people to be good citizens and encourage them to develop into well-rounded people, there are far healthier ways of doing it than locking them into their studies at a formative time of their lives and forcing them to compete in a 'points race'.

Yours etc.
D. Murphy
D. Murphy
Sparrow Close
Cork

Comment

- **Audience**: Readers of the newspaper are clearly the **audience** for this letter. From this it follows that the **context** is public rather than private. Although the actual **content** of the letter was not specified, the instruction was to write 'on a subject that concerns young people', which the Leaving Cert does.

- **Register**: Language is formal, as appropriate for the context and the topic. The writer chooses the **language of argument** to make the case that the 'points race' is damaging to young people and suggests alternative methods for admission to college. Other features of this **genre of language** include asking questions, making strong statements and supporting arguments with illustrations.

- Emotive phrases and exaggeration for effect, which are features of the **language of persuasion**, help to support the main argument.

- **Form**: Opening/closing greeting conventions are included. There are three paragraphs, each with its own **topic sentence** or main point.

Example 2: Report

Write a report for your local council on facilities for young people in your area.

Title of report: Youth Facilities in Anytown

Date: 12 June 2007

Terms of reference

This report was commissioned by Anytown District Council to investigate facilities for young people in the Anytown area with a view to upgrading.

Research

A working group of five people was established. Each member visited a number of amenities. A questionnaire was given to a representative group of young people in the area.

Findings

- Sports amenities comprise two football pitches, one for Gaelic football and one for soccer, and one indoor basketball court in the small community hall.

- The community hall is also available for groups such as Scouts and Girl Guides to meet. Apart from the basketball court, facilities such as access to sports equipment are poor. The roof of the hall is in need of repair.

- The youth club meets in a room in the local primary school, St Margaret's. Activities there are curtailed due to severe lack of space. Desks and tables must be constantly rearranged, with consequent damage to school equipment.

Results of survey

- 90 per cent of those surveyed considered amenities for young people to be 'inadequate'.

- 85 per cent highlighted the poor provision of sports facilities, especially for girls.

- 80 per cent deplored the lack of a swimming pool in the area.

- 70 per cent considered that the local hall should also be available to the youth club.

Recommendations

- Planning permission should be obtained and budgetary concerns addressed for the provision of a purpose-built recreation centre with suitable facilities.

- A swimming pool should be included in the plans.

- Surveys should be conducted on an ongoing basis to monitor local views.

Conclusion

The working group would like to thank all those who participated in the survey. We would hope that Anytown District Council will give urgent consideration to the matter of facilities for young people in their area.

Signed: *Linda Johnson*
(on behalf of the working group)

Top Tip

REVISE WISE
POINTS TO NOTE

Be aware of the choice of synonyms open to you. For example, *participate* is more formal than *take part in*. Choose appropriately!

Comment

- **Audience**: A report of this kind is a **formal text** which will be read primarily by those who have commissioned it.

- **Register**: Language is formal and impersonal. Its **purpose is to inform** and also to draw conclusions from the information, i.e. to recommend a particular course of action.

- As in the **language of information**, the emphasis is on **clarity and order**. There is little personal opinion offered.

- **Form**: The structure is clear: **Terms of Reference, Research, Findings, Recommendations, Conclusion**.

Examination section

Each of the **three** comprehension texts is followed by a **Question B**, the functional writing task.

- Read **all** of the texts before you choose to answer comprehension questions on **one** of them (Question A).

- Take note of **Question B** which follows each text. One of them may appeal more to you than the others.

- **Remember**, you must **not** answer Question A and B on the same text. However, the text may be useful or even essential for you in your own piece of writing. Use it as a resource.

- As you read the question, it is a good idea to highlight key words, making sure you have a clear idea of what you are being asked to do.

- Plan your answer before you begin. Think about the **purpose, audience, register, form** and **context**, as explained above.

- You are not asked for a lengthy piece of writing in Question B. In recent years, the examination paper has not specified any particular length. For 50 marks, it would seem reasonable to write approximately **one to one and a half pages**.

Total marks for Comprehending, Paper 1, Question B	Time suggested
50	35 minutes

Sample question and answer 1: Diary entries

Paper 1, Text 1, Leaving Cert 2005

(Note: You should read the original passage, *An Ordinary Life*, and sample comprehension question in Chapter 2, p. 34.)

'On Saturday afternoons Margaret Ann would go to the market to buy the meat for Sunday.'

Write **three diary entries** that Margaret Ann might have written over a series of Saturday evenings. Your writing should relate to her experience as described in the passage.

Before you begin to write:

- Read the passage again. Remember, you will **not** have chosen to answer comprehension questions on it.

- The instructions clearly state that the diary entries should **relate to her experience as described in the passage**. So whereas you are free to introduce some new aspects of her experience, they should be in keeping with the passage itself.

Sample answer

Saturday, 10 June 1890

Exhausted again tonight. Mrs S. always so fussy about everything, though I do like a tidy house myself. That Annie is so demanding. Wish she'd find the rich husband she's looking for! Then I wouldn't have to wash and starch her clothes all the time.

Only good part of the day today was visiting the market for the Sunday meat. At least it gets me out of the house on Saturdays. That Thomas Hind keeps a good stall, I must say. Everything spotless. Always very polite too. Not too familiar like some of the others I could mention. I met his sisters, Mollie and Cissie, last week at church – nice respectable girls. Wonder if he's walking out with anyone?

Saturday, 17 June

Some of the customers at the market have no manners, pushing in front of you like that. But Thomas Hind always serves everyone in turn. Heard Jenny from No. 12 telling someone that Hind's stall does very well – makes enough to keep his mother and two sisters as well as himself. Must be a good manager. I like the look of him (now don't lose the run of yourself, Margaret Ann, as mother used to say!). But he has nice brown hair and lovely eyes. And today I thought he was especially polite, asking me whether I like the hot weather we're having and if I found sea air refreshing. Told him I did.

Saturday, 24 June

Something great has happened! Can hardly believe it. Thomas Hind asked me on an outing with himself and his sisters to Burgh marsh! Said he wondered if I was free next Sunday. We're going on the omnibus out to the promenade at Burgh to have tea before taking a breath of sea air. What will I wear? Maybe my blue bonnet and cloak?

Will have to learn to call him Thomas now – or is it Tom?

Comment

- Like the passage it is based on, the **genre** of writing here is **narrative**, so it will tell a story of some kind – in this case, a brief romantic story about the beginning of a relationship. Even though the story is brief, there is a clear **beginning**, **development** and **conclusion**.

- **Context**: The diary of a servant girl in 1890s England. Based on the original passage, Margaret Ann's diary reveals that she is **hard-working**, with **high standards of cleanliness and behaviour**.

- References to *starch*, *omnibus*, *bonnet* also help to give a sense of context – a **setting** in which the story takes place.

- A diary is a **private** rather than **public** piece of writing, so comments and reflections on what happens are to be expected – in this case, cautious revelations of an interest in Thomas Hind.

- The **register** is not too formal. The language is **elliptical**, i.e. **I** is omitted at the beginning of sentences. But it maintains the sense of correctness that seems to be a part of the writer's character.

Top Tip

Diary entries are among examiners' favourite questions. Depending on the context, it may be acceptable to write in a very colloquial style – exactly as the character would speak – but bear in mind that you are still writing for an examiner, so always avoid any offensive language or references.

Sample question and answer 2

Text 1, Question B, Leaving Cert 2004

'Then along comes school.'

You have been asked to give a short talk to a group of students who are about to start first year in your school. Write out the text of the talk you would give.

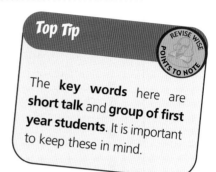

Top Tip

The **key words** here are **short talk** and **group of first year students**. It is important to keep these in mind.

Sample answer

Well here you all are, looking very smart, I must say, in your new uniforms. You're probably feeling a bit nervous – I remember I did when I started. You've just come from primary school where you were the 'big girls and boys' to the secondary, where as you've no doubt noticed, some of the sixth years are over six feet tall! But the first thing I want to say is that here at St Rita's we try to make everyone feel welcome.

I'm Anne Walsh, this year's Head Girl. I'm not going to give you a long talk about what to do or what not to do in school. Your form teachers will go over all that. But I do have one or two words of advice for you. Try to get to know as many new people as you can. Everyone will tell you that friends help to make school more enjoyable. A great way to make friends is to take part in as many activities as you can. We have football, hurling and basketball teams as well as the drama club and the computer club, so you won't be stuck for things to do.

We have a good prefect system at St Rita's as well. There are six senior students on the prefects' committee and we are here to help you. We all remember that when we were in first year it was often easier to tell another pupil about any problems we had rather than our parents or teachers, so if you're feeling confused or upset about anything, or simply want to have a chat, you can come to any one of us and hopefully we can help.

I'm going to finish now by wishing you all well in your school days here at St Rita's. It's a great school and we're all very proud of it. Enjoy every minute of your time here. Believe me, it'll fly!

Comment

- The 'short talk' falls into the **genre** of the **language of persuasion**, e.g. you want the audience to react in a certain way. There will also be elements of the **language of information** (the students will need to be told something about the school).

- Friendly, informal tone addresses audience directly: 'Well here you all are.'

- Contains some information about sports teams, clubs, prefects.

- Refers to feelings of audience: 'You're probably feeling a bit nervous.'

- The choice of language (**register**) is informal ('stuck for things to do', 'it'll fly'), but the **context** is still relatively formal and public rather than private – the speaker is representing the school authorities rather than simply giving her own private views.

- The **form** of the speech, i.e. its shape, follows a clear pattern: **introductory remarks** (words of welcome), followed by **body of talk** (information about school). **Conclusion** appeals to feelings and includes everyone in a general way.

Sample question and answer 3

Paper 1, Text 3, Question B, Leaving Cert 2005

Imagine that as a reporter for a local newspaper you plan to interview a celebrity of your choice. Write a proposal/memo for the editor of your newspaper in which you explain why you want to interview this celebrity, giving an outline of the areas you hope to explore in the course of the interview.

Before you begin:

- A memo is a short text that is usually sent within an organisation or company.

- As a reporter on the newspaper, you obviously work with the editor (**context**).

- Therefore, the **register** you use should be business-like. However, it is appropriate to be reasonably friendly in this situation.

- You want the editor to agree to a proposal. It follows that your memo/proposal falls into the language genre of **information** and **persuasion**.

Sample answer

Memo

To:	Mr James O'Hara
From:	Mark Riley
Date:	15 August 2007
Re:	Proposed interview with Colin Farrell

James,

I've just heard that the actor Colin Farrell is to be at home in Castleknock shortly. I think this is a golden opportunity to interview him, as our paper serves the Dublin 15 area and he is our 'local boy made good'. I think our readers would be very interested in what he has to say.

I'd hope to explore the following areas with him:

- His schooldays in Dublin 15: did he have any opportunity to act? Who or what influenced him to be an actor?

- His favourite haunts in the area? Any unusual memories/anecdotes?

- His career to date: how he began, what has been his greatest achievement, his present film project.

> **Comment**
>
> Note the **form** of the memo – it makes use of **bullet points** to convey information as succinctly as possible.

- His relationships with his fellow actors and the persistent rumours about his love life.

- His opinion of Hollywood and the glamour of show business.

- His plans for the future, both professional and personal.

- Any words of wisdom for aspiring young actors.

I estimate the interview will be about 1,000 words. Please let me know as soon as possible if I have the go-ahead, as I'd need to contact his agent and arrange for John to take photographs of Colin.

Regards,
Mark

Practice Questions

1 **Advertising and young people – You report to the Advertising Standards Authority**. There is much discussion as to whether or not young people are being exploited by advertisers. Write a short report to the Advertising Standards Authority outlining your views on the matter. **(LC 2006)**

2 Write a letter to a photographic magazine in which you propose **one** of the four images of *Ordinary Lives in War Time* (see Chapter 2, p. 39) for the award '**Best War Photograph of the Year**'. **(LC 2005)**

3 Imagine that you have discovered a time capsule containing a number of items from the distant **or** more recent past. Write a letter to a local or national newspaper announcing your find and describing the items contained in the capsule. **(LC 2004)**

4 The Holiday from Hell: Write three or four diary entries that record the details of a disastrous holiday (real or imaginary) that you experienced. **(LC 2003)**

5 'Rights Must Be Observed': You have been asked to give a short talk on radio or television about a fundamental human right you would like to see supported more strongly. Write out the text of the talk you would give. **(LC 2002)**

6 Write a short article about a project or activity in your local community which you admire or condemn. **(LC 2001)**

7 Write a review for a **young people's magazine** of a film you have enjoyed.

8 You wish to sell a **historic castle** you have inherited. Write the text of an advertisement for the castle, to appear in the property pages of a newspaper.

9 You are a civil servant. Write a **memo** for the Minister for Health suggesting how the problem of obesity might be tackled.

10 Write a set of **guidelines** for care and safety in the countryside, to be displayed in your local forest park.

11 Write a series of diary entries (at least **three**) of a week in the life of a Leaving Certificate student.

Remember

- **Question B is worth 50 marks.**
- As in all sections of the exam, remember to **plan, write, check**.

Key Points

- Comprehending, Paper 1, Question B tests your knowledge of how language works in a variety of situations.

- Be prepared to write in any of the five genres of language.

- Take into account **purpose**, **audience**, **context**, **register** and **form**.

- Read instructions very carefully, underlining **key words**.

- Remember to **plan**, **write**, **check**.

- Suggested time for Comprehending, Paper 1, Question B: **35 minutes**.

- **Total marks** for Question B: **50**.

4: Composing

●●● Learning Objectives

In this chapter you will learn:

● How to plan and write different types of composition.

Introduction

Paper 1, Section II, Composing is worth 100 marks – 25 per cent of all the marks allotted for the exam. It is the longest single piece of writing you will have to do, so it is important that you write as well as you can.

The process of writing has **three parts: planning, writing** and **checking**.

Planning

● In most instances the **title** of the essay and the key **task words** (words that tell you what to do with the content) will suggest the shape and register of your composition, e.g. write a **short story**, write a **speech**, write an **article for a newspaper**.

● Other titles may invite you to write a **personal essay**, where you have to decide for yourself what you want your piece of writing to do – entertain, persuade, describe – always keeping yourself and your feelings at the centre.

● But whatever title you choose to write about, it is essential to make a **plan** before you write. It will give you a sense of what shape your composition will take – and make it clearer for the examiner, too.

Suggestions for making a plan

1. Brainstorming.

● Write the title of your essay in the centre of the page. Underneath, make a list of all the words/ideas you can think of about your chosen topic. Don't try to put them in any order at this stage.

- Next, make another list in which you **cluster** words/ideas which seem to connect. These may eventually form your paragraphs.

- You may then be ready to begin to write.

2. Make a mind-map.

- If you have a brain that works best visually, you might find a diagram or mind-map helpful in planning. Again, write the title of your essay in the centre of the page. Write down your word and idea associations in a map pattern, one leading to the next. This can help you see connections between ideas, as if you were seeing a landscape from the air.

See examples of both methods on pp. 64–5.

Writing the essay: Putting your ideas in order

The planning stages mentioned above are for discovering what your ideas are for your topic. You must then decide what order to put them in. It helps to keep in mind that every piece of writing shares the same **three-part structure:**

- **Introduction.**

- **Body (middle).**

- **Conclusion.**

Each of these parts requires careful consideration if you are to give your essay a sense of coherence and unity.

Introduction

Avoid boring openings that merely repeat what the topic of the essay is. Some suggestions for beginning an essay include the following.

- Ask a question that will involve the reader from the start: 'Are you a mobile phone junkie?' (Feature article discussing the popularity of mobile phones.)

- Begin with an anecdote (a brief story), making sure it doesn't go on too long and makes its point clear as soon as possible: 'My neighbour John has lived on our road for 50 years. He has always been friendly with everyone,

watching out for them and their families. Recently, some boys broke through his front window and forced him to hand over his money. And I'm sorry to say that he has since lost the will to live. His faith in his fellow human beings has gone.' (Essay illustrating the effects of petty crime on elderly people.)

- A sincere and personal statement of your intentions can be effective, too: 'My mother died last year and I would like to tell you about her.' (Personal essay about family relationships.)

- A strong, provocative statement will help to convince the reader of your views: 'I am always amazed when I hear people saying that sport is always a force for good in society, when clearly the world of sport is riddled with corruption and violence.'

- In a short story, the opening sentence should arouse the reader's interest: 'Murphy knew they were following him.'

Body (middle)

The body of the essay is where you develop, paragraph by paragraph, the points you want to make. At this stage your plan should be useful in keeping your essay relevant, making sure you don't go off the point.

- You will need to decide whether you will begin with what you think is the most important point, or lead up to it as the essay proceeds.

- In essays written mainly in the **language of narration**, or short stories in which language is used in an **aesthetic** way, you may need to decide the time sequence of events: will there be a **chronological order**? Will you begin mid-way through the story, or even, as sometimes happens, at the end, making use of **flashbacks**?

- Whichever order you choose, each new aspect of the story/situation requires a new paragraph.

Top Tips

- There is no hard and fast rule about the length of paragraphs. A fast-paced short story or personal narrative may have short paragraphs of a couple of sentences. Paragraphs in essays written to inform, argue or persuade usually require longer development – about one-third to half of an A4 page is acceptable.

- For essays written mainly to **inform**, **argue** or **persuade**, each paragraph should contain a **topic** or **thesis sentence**, where the main idea in the paragraph is made clear. The point can then be developed by further details about it, as well as illustrations, statistics/facts, supporting ideas. (See example on pp. 66–7.)

- Be careful to **link paragraphs** by using **connectives**. This helps to show **clarity of purpose** and **coherence**, two of the main criteria by which the essay is assessed.

Here are some ways of **linking paragraphs**:

- Echo the key words and ideas of the final sentence of the previous paragraph.

- Repeat sentence patterns of the previous paragraph.

- Commonly used linking words:
  - ❖ To show you are adding to the point: *and, furthermore, what is more, moreover.*
  - ❖ Making a contrast: *but, however, on the other hand, it's true that, admittedly.*
  - ❖ Suggesting consequence: *as a result, so, therefore, consequently.*
  - ❖ Giving examples: *for example, for instance, to put this more clearly.*

Conclusion

Just like your opening paragraph, the **conclusion** of your essay leaves the examiner with a distinct impression that you have managed to say what you had to say as efficiently as possible.

Avoid allowing your essay to just fizzle out, as if you were simply tired of writing.

Suggestions for concluding your composition:

- Answer the question you asked in the first sentence.

- Go back to your original statement and echo it in some way.

- Create a vivid image that encapsulates what you have been saying in the essay.

- An effective short story might have a 'twist in the tail' or surprise ending (something is finally revealed).

- An apt quotation can be impressive, but difficult to produce in an exam situation.

Writing the essay: Example

Now let's put these suggestions into practice in an example.

'Celebrity culture has gone too far.'

Write a *speech* in which you attempt to *persuade* an audience that today's obsession with the lives of the rich and famous has gone too far. (LC 2005)

- Clearly, the key words here are those in *italics*: speech, persuade. These words suggest the shape and register of your writing.

- The content has also been outlined: obsession with celebrity culture.

Example of brainstorming

- role models – 15 minutes of fame – self-delusion – vulnerable people

- websites – magazines – fanzines – lack of self-esteem – loss of identity

- anorexia – drugs – human beings – paparazzi – not new – big business – stress

- Princess Diana – the Beatles – Charles Dickens – Celebrity Big Brother – the future?

Next, attempt to cluster similar ideas together:

1. Role models: How vulnerable young people see the rich and famous. Possible bad effects – anorexia, drug-taking.

2. Whole magazines (*Heat*), entire websites devoted to the rich and famous. Rise of fanzines (magazines entirely about particular celebrity). Power of media/paparazzi – big business.

3. Do we reveal lack of self-esteem/sense of identity in our worship of celebrity culture?

4. Young people delude themselves – want 15 minutes of fame – shows like *You're a Star*, *Pop Idol*, etc.

5. Celebrities are themselves human – tragedies occur – Princess Diana, stress, etc.

6. May not be new phenomenon – Charles Dickens mobbed in America, the Beatles in the 1960s, etc.

7. What about the future?

Even though you may decide to change the order above, these seven aspects of the topic will form the basis of your paragraphs. You now have a workable plan.

Example of mind-map

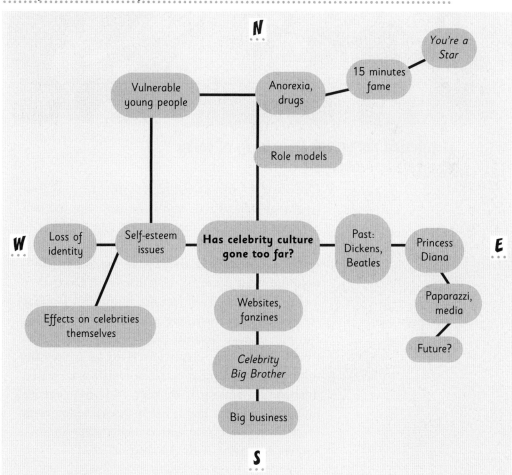

Suggested opening

Shows awareness of audience. Links past with present. Asks relevant question which speech will try to answer.

When I was invited to speak to you tonight about our obsession with celebrity culture, I found myself thinking that this obsession has, to an extent, existed for a long time. You might be surprised to hear me saying this. But we have evidence that people were fascinated by celebrities in the past. Charles Dickens was mobbed by an enthusiastic crowd when he first visited America in the nineteenth century. In the 1960s, the Beatles were hounded by the press and chased by screaming teenagers. What, then, you might ask, is different about today?

Suggested paragraph from body of essay

Topic sentence at beginning of paragraph is supported by illustration and development.

One aspect of celebrity culture that I find particularly disturbing, and I feel sure that you will all agree with me, is the influence that the lifestyle of celebrities can have on vulnerable young people. Jennifer Aniston or Britney Spears has lost weight – hold the front cover of *Heat* magazine! Don't they look great in the latest Versace outfit! But Jennifer or Britney's fitness regime may not be appropriate for the average second year student, who now thinks she has to starve herself to keep up with these people. In recent years anorexia has increased dramatically, among both boys and girls, and it's interesting to note that it has increased in line with the growing obsession with celebrity culture in our society. Never mind that adolescents need plenty of nourishment for good health. Body image is all.

Linking paragraph

Link made by 'and' (addition to point) as well as repetition of key word 'image'.

> And whose body image is it? Is it the image created by the media, whose power to influence even celebrities themselves is immense? (etc.)

Conclusion

Final paragraph asks question and appeals to emotions. Final sentence leaves audience with idea to consider.

> I am sure that some of you are sitting here saying to yourselves, why doesn't she lighten up? Is our interest in the lives of the rich and famous not simply a form of harmless escapism? But having listened to what I have had to say about the dangers of our obsession, is this attitude just a little naïve? Ladies and gentlemen, I urge you to consider that in our anxiety to know all about the lifestyle of celebrities and, even more, to imitate them, we are in danger of losing what is precious to all of us – a sense of our own identity as individuals in this world.

Checking

Proofreading or checking your work is **essential**. You will spot at least some mistakes if you reread the essay carefully.

Common errors include:

- Omitting endings of words.

- Confusing homonyms, i.e. words that sound the same but have different meanings and are spelled differently, such as alter/altar, pier/peer.

- Grammatical errors such as non-agreement of noun and verb, e.g. 'There's two sides to this story' (incorrect) instead of 'There are two sides to this story' (correct).

- There may be certain words that you constantly misspell. As you revise, compile a list of these words. Focus on the correct spelling and watch out for them in the exam.

- Having checked your work for possible errors in spelling and grammar, read it again with punctuation in mind.

- Allow five minutes for rereading your essay.

The personal essay

A personal essay gives you freedom to approach a topic in whichever way you choose, but with one requirement: that there is a clear personal voice or viewpoint. Make the 'I' the centre of what you write.

The two examples that follow illustrate two different approaches to the personal essay. Both were written by young people and published in the 'TeenTimes' column in *The Irish Times*.

Example 1

The Filth and the Fury, by Luíseach nic Eoin, deals with a familiar family situation.

She has been nagging me about it for weeks. You know how it is, every single conversation you have meandering down the same route, ending in 'when'?

Take morning time, for example.

Child: (brightly): 'Good morning, Mother, you slept well, I trust?'

Mother (darkly and gloweringly): 'Clean it.'

Or after coming home from another weary day at your summer job.

Child (wearily): 'I had a load of nightmare customers again! How was your day?'

Mother (with a murderous glint in her eye): 'I mean it. Clean your room this instant or I'm going to the tabloids and telling them about the miraculous new bacterial life-forms living in a surprisingly advanced civilisation on that bowl of Rice Krispies under your bed.'

Child (meekly): 'Yes ma'am. Yes ma'am, right after I've finished my game of Spider Solitaire on the computer. Oh come on, the organisms are hardly advanced – they haven't even developed satellite TV yet or built their own iPods. I'll do it later.'

Except, that doesn't really work out, and somehow hours later you're still on the sofa watching *Irish Paint Magic*, and steam is coming out of your mother's ears. As you toddle off to bed for a well-earned rest, did you imagine it or did she really cackle and say 'I'll get you tomorrow, my pretty'?

Ahh. First day of the weekend, a break from your hard-working slog, the time is about 11 a.m. You stretch out in bed and incline your head slightly to see what a beautiful sunny day it is – children playing on swings, kittens gambolling in the garden.

Oh wait. It's actually 7 degrees and the hail is pelting down onto the sodden little kittens' backs.

Oh well, you think, another seven hours in bed, and it'll have cleared up enough for me to get up.

But Mammy dear has other ideas. Just as you roll over, you hear a faint, creeping footstep, which is actually more of a sticky trudge, reminding you that you hadn't quite gotten round to clearing up that Nutella and nail varnish that had been spilled on the floor.

Then a sopping wet face cloth hits you square on the face. You scream, but it's too late – she has already yanked the bedclothes off your pathetic pyjama-clad body and has left the room cackling about the pit of despair and the vortex under the bed.

Unfortunately, the evil fairy effect is spoiled somewhat when she trips over a pile of magazines and lands with her head in a bowl of stale cereal. Ooops.

As the mother departs, limping slightly and threatening to call social services, you decide you may as well get up and watch TV. Unfortunately, with the first step out of bed, you turn on a hairdryer with your foot. Hmm.

Perhaps she had a point. If you cleaned out the room you could open up the vortex under the bed to tourists.

And you know, NASA probably would be interested in the way that spilled hair gel and toothpaste combined appears to defy several laws of thermodynamics.

My room could be a tourist attraction to rival Newgrange with people queuing around the block to marvel at my scientist-confounding mess.

It could. Or I could just go back to bed.

Comment

- Luíseach's essay has a basic **narrative shape** as she creates a humorous situation of mother-daughter conflict. There is a clear **setting** (the home), **time** (summer, working days, weekends) and **progression** (beginning of conflict, how it develops, ending with anti-climax: 'I could just go back to bed').

- She creates two distinct characters, the mother and the daughter, building up their roles in the narrative with techniques belonging to the **aesthetic use of language**, for example, dialogue.

- She makes use of **hyperbole (deliberate exaggeration)** and **absurd images** (mother as 'cackling' witch, falling over bowl of cereal, etc.) for humorous effect.

- Informal words like 'oops', 'hmm', etc. add to our sense of someone thinking aloud, giving the essay its personal tone.

- Writers are often advised to 'show, don't tell'. Instead of saying 'dirt on the floor', there is 'Nutella and nail varnish', a concrete image that is far more descriptive.

- Notice, too, how the writer links paragraphs, e.g. the word 'could' is echoed through the final paragraphs and emphasised for effect in the last sentence.

Source: Luíseach nic Eoin, *The Irish Times*, 30 August 2005

Example 2

Elaine Lynch has a very personal take on the subject of school uniforms.

We are not uniform individuals

Come with my imagination into this iron house that some would call a school and picture with me this scene.

A girl, no more than 15, is backed against a wall, on the verge of tears as a teacher bellows at her, spittle flying in all directions, her face going a shade of red that would shame a traffic light, as she rants and raves with no sign of stopping.

Now what was this girl's crime, you ask? Surely she must have done something truly heinous to deserve this vicious assault? Perhaps she has been caught smoking in the toilets or using her mobile? Did she 'forget' her homework for the umpteenth time?

No, I am sorry to tell you that her crime was far more dreadful than this, she was caught…wearing make-up! Oh yes, this little second or third year is having her face bitten off because she was wearing make-up. And her skirt was the wrong length, her shoes were too high, she was wearing far too much jewellery…the list goes on. The endless rules that schools give their pupils for appearance are totally ridiculous and uncalled for. Why must everyone look the same? What business is it of theirs whether people wear make-up or not? Or, in the case of boys' schools, what length they wear their hair? How does what the pupils look like affect how much they learn? Answer me that and I will happily bow to all of your petty rules. Until then, I have a few things to get off my chest.

First things first, let's start with the biggest issue – make-up. Schools don't like us to wear make-up because it is considered by them to be 'distracting'. Distracting to whom? In case you hadn't noticed we're an all-girls' school. There are many arguments for and against make-up in general, but I believe it should be up to the individual to make up, if you'll excuse the atrocious pun, their own mind. Many girls feel extremely self-conscious about the way they look and need to wear make-up to feel good about themselves, and who are the schools to take that away? What right have they to make someone feel ugly?

Some girls wear it to cover up acne or scars, others still wear it purely for the fun of experimenting with colour. Make-up makes all these girls happy in one way or another, but still, schools try to stamp it out – even though it has no impact whatsoever on what we learn. In fact, I would nearly go so far as to say that it has a detrimental effect, as it makes the pupils unhappy.

Secondly, the skirt. Who honestly cares what length people's skirts are? It's their own decision, surely. But oh no, schools have to try to control that too. Well let me say this, if you don't like the way we wear our skirts, give us the option of trousers. Do they have any idea how uncomfortable and inconvenient skirts are? Too hot in summer, too cold in winter and no protection whatsoever from the rain. And tights. They are the biggest nuisance you will ever come across. When you need a pair every one you find will have ladders in it.

All of this hassle could be avoided if we were allowed to wear trousers. From a practical point of view, just imagine how warm they would be in winter. I'm not even against school uniforms. I think they have their purpose, just like any other piece of clothing. I'm merely against the unenlightened idea that girls must wear skirts, and boys wear trousers.

Next, the jewellery issue. Jewellery is also considered 'distracting'. Unless you have a human magpie in class I will go ahead and call this a load of nonsense, too. Do you really think we students are so idiotic as to go 'Ooh, shiny!' when we see a piece of 'distracting' jewellery? And as for heels, well, we all know the reason for that one is insurance.

However, what really bothers me about this scenario is not the rules themselves so much as the fact that a human being should have the power to stifle the personality and individuality of others. I opened this piece with a slightly altered quote from Patrick Kavanagh as he was a man who knew all about individuality. He was a lone voice in his time, and that is why I wrote this piece, because I feel the pupils of Ireland should be given a voice.

Students should be allowed to look whatever way they want to look and no one should be able to change that. Have you ever noticed how teachers can wear enough make-up to bury the city and earrings that could take someone's eye out and yet nobody berates them to the point of tears?

I say individuality before conformity. If they want an army of clones sitting before them then they can go and join the Dolly the sheep research project.

Source: Elaine Lynch, *The Irish Times*, 20 December 2005

Comment

- Elaine's essay has a strong personal tone throughout as she expresses her opinions about the issue of school uniforms: 'The endless rules that schools give their pupils for appearance are totally ridiculous and uncalled for.'

- Instead of a narrative approach, she opts to write primarily in the **language of argument**.

- Her opening paragraph vividly illustrates the problems that defying the school uniform rule poses for students.

- She raises relevant questions: 'Why must everyone look the same?', 'How does what the pupils look like affect what they will learn?'

- She then answers these questions in the course of the essay.

- The linking phrases give a sense of coherence and logic to her arguments: 'First things first', 'Secondly', 'all of this', 'Next', 'However'.

- The final sentence is particularly effective – the image of Dolly the sheep encapsulates the stifling of individuality that she sees in schools.

The short story

Writing a short story involves writing in the **language of narration**. You are telling a story, with a beginning, middle and end.

It also involves the **aesthetic use of language**, which students sometimes find difficult. It requires some attempt to create the following features of a short story:

- Setting.

- Credible characters that offer the reader some psychological insight.

- A crucial moment which gives the reader an insight into the meaning of the story or situation of the characters (called an 'epiphany' by James Joyce).

- A resolution or some sense of closure.

The short story writer must make decisions about whether to write in the **first person, I,** or the **third person he/she** (see Chapter 1, pp. 19–20). **Dialogue** helps to bring characters alive for the reader, too.

We can see some of these techniques at work in the following short story by the celebrated Irish writer Liam O'Flaherty.

His First Flight

The young seagull was alone on his ledge. His two brothers and his sister had already flown away the day before. He had been afraid to fly with them. Somehow when he had taken a little run forward to the brink of the ledge and attempted to flap his wings he became afraid. The great expanse of sea stretched down beneath, and it was such a long way down – miles down. He felt certain that his wings would never support him, so he bent his head and ran away back to the little hole under the ledge where he slept at night. Even when each of his brothers and his little sister, whose wings were far shorter than his own, ran to the brink, flapped their wings, and flew away, he failed to muster up courage to take that plunge which appeared to him so desperate. His father and mother had come around calling to him shrilly, upbraiding him, threatening to let him starve on his ledge unless he flew away. But for the life of him he could not move.

That was twenty-four hours ago. Since then nobody had come near him. The day before, all day long, he had watched his parents flying about with his brothers and sister, perfecting them in the art of flight, teaching them how to skim the waves and how to dive for fish. He had, in fact, seen his older brother catch his first herring and devour it, standing on a rock, while his parents circled around raising a proud cackle. And all the morning the whole family had walked about on the big plateau midway down the opposite cliff, taunting him with his cowardice.

The sun was now ascending the sky, blazing warmly on his ledge that faced the south. He felt the heat because he had not eaten since the previous nightfall. Then he had found a dried piece of mackerel's tail at the far end of his ledge. Now there was not a single scrap of food left. He had searched every inch, rooting among the rough, dirt-caked straw nest where he and his brothers and sister had been hatched. He even gnawed at the dried pieces of spotted eggshell. It was like eating part of himself. He had then trotted back and forth from one end of the ledge to the other, his grey body the colour of the cliff, his long grey legs stepping daintily, trying to find some means

of reaching his parents without having to fly. But on each side of him the ledge ended in a sheer fall of precipice, with the sea beneath. And between him and his parents there was a deep, wide chasm. Surely he could reach them without flying if he could only move northwards along the cliff face? But then on what could he walk? There was no ledge, and he was not a fly. And above him he could see nothing. The precipice was sheer, and the top of it was perhaps farther away than the sea beneath him.

He stepped slowly out to the brink of the ledge, and, standing on one leg with the other hidden under his wing, he closed one eye, then the other, and pretended to be falling asleep. Still they took no notice of him. He saw his two brothers and his sister lying on the plateau, her white breast thrust forward. Now and again she tore at a piece of fish that lay at her feet, and then scraped each side of her beak on the rock. The sight of the food maddened him. How he loved to tear food that way, scraping his beak now and again to whet it! He uttered a low cackle. His mother cackled too, and looked over at him.

'Ga, ga, ga,' he cried, begging her to bring him over some food. 'Gaw-ool-ah,' she screamed back derisively. But he kept calling plaintively, and after a minute or so he uttered a joyful scream. His mother had picked up a piece of the fish and was flying across to him with it. He leaned out eagerly tapping the rock with his feet, trying to get nearer to her as she flew across. But when she was just opposite to him, abreast of the ledge, she halted, her leg hanging limp, her wings motionless, the piece of fish in her beak almost within reach of his beak. He waited a moment in surprise, wondering why she did not come nearer, and then, maddened by hunger, he dived at the fish. With a loud scream he fell outwards and downwards into space. His mother had swooped upwards. As he passed beneath her he heard the swish of her wings. Then a monstrous terror seized him and his heart stood still. He could hear nothing. But it only lasted a moment. The next moment he felt his wings spread outwards. The wind rushed against his breast feathers, then under his stomach and against his wings. He could feel the tips of his wings cutting through the air. He was not falling headlong now. He was soaring gradually downwards and outwards. He was no longer afraid. He just felt a bit dizzy. Then he flapped his wings once and he soared upwards. He uttered a joyous scream and flapped them again. 'Ga, ga, ga. Ga, ga, ga. Gaw-ool-ah.' His mother swooped past him, her wings making a loud noise. He answered her with another scream. Then his father flew over him screaming. Then he saw his two brothers and sister flying around him curvetting and banking and soaring and diving.

Then he completely forgot that he had not always been able to fly, and commenced himself to dive and soar and curvet, shrieking shrilly.

He was near the sea now, flying straight over it, facing straight out over the ocean. He saw a vast green sea beneath him, with little ridges moving over it, and he turned his beak sideways and crowed amusedly. His parents and his brothers and sister had landed on this green floor in front of him. They were beckoning to him, calling shrilly. He dropped his legs to stand on the green sea. His legs sank into it. He screamed with fright and attempted to rise again, flapping his wings. But he was tired and weak with hunger and he could not rise, exhausted by the strange exercise. His feet sank into the green sea, and then his belly touched it and he sank farther. He was floating on it. And around him his family was screaming, praising him, and their beaks were offering him scraps of dog-fish.

He had made his first flight.

- **Paragraph 1**: Scene is set. Characters (non-human) introduced. Problem/conflict suggested: 'But for the life of him he could not move.'

- **Paragraph 2**: Flashback to earlier time. Characters developed.

- **Paragraph 3**: Complications developing – nothing to eat. Seagull's response to dilemma described. Further description of setting.

- **Paragraph 4**: Relationship between mother/young seagull developed. Situation building towards climax: mother/son confront each other.

- **Paragraph 5**: Crisis point in story. Action of mother creates situation that brings about solution to problem. Young seagull's response described in detail. Insight into psychology of flying.

- **Paragraph 6/7**: Sense of closure: problem is resolved. Last sentence sums up theme of story.

Top Tip

Examiners do not look for a professionally written short story, but they are asked to **reward awareness of narrative shape**.

Examination section

- The total time allotted for Paper 1 is **2 hours 50 minutes (170 minutes)**.

- As suggested in earlier chapters, you are advised to answer Section I (Comprehending) first, as the texts are a valuable resource for both Question B (the functional writing task) and Section II, Composing.

A suggested **breakdown of your time** is:

- 20 minutes to read and choose questions.

- 35 minutes on Question A in Section I, Comprehending.

- 35 minutes on Question B in Section I, Comprehending.

- 80 minutes on your composition in Section II, Composing (allowing 15 minutes for planning and five minutes for checking).

At the top of the page, the following statement appears: *The composition assignments below are intended to reflect language study in the areas of information, argument, persuasion, narration and the aesthetic use of language.*

- Bear in mind that these language genres continually mingle within texts, but pay attention to the **main purpose** of your composition.

- The choice of titles offered (usually seven or eight) is based on the **general theme** of the paper.

- For each title, there is a title or quotation taken from the comprehension texts, and an instruction or task word. Read it carefully, underlining key words.

Top Tip

Key words will give you the context (serious journal, school magazine), **form** (speech, article, short story) and **purpose** (persuade, argue, discuss) of your essay. You will then have to decide on the most appropriate register.

- **Remember**, some instructions are more prescriptive than others. If you are asked to *argue* a particular case for a *serious journal*, you will not have the same freedom of choice as you would have for a *personal essay* or *features article*.

- Even though a composition title is linked to one of the texts, you are free to refer to or draw ideas from **any or all of the texts and their accompanying illustrations**.

- You need not refer to any of the texts, however – you may prefer to write from your own knowledge or experience.

- There is no definite **length** specified for the composition. Many students write between 750–1,000 words in the time available.

- There are **100 marks** allotted for the composition.

Total marks for Composing	Time suggested
100	80 minutes

Practice Questions

1 'It was mad…Ridiculous.'
   Write a short story suggested by the above title. **(LC 2006)**

2 'Imagine it's St. Valentine's Day…' Write an article for a popular magazine on the importance of romance in our lives. **(LC 2006)**

3 'My take on recent history.' Write a personal essay in which you discuss your views on a recent event or series of events in the world. **(LC 2005)**

4 'The hope that things will be better for the next generation.' Write an article for a newspaper or magazine, outlining your vision of a better future. **(LC 2005)**

5 Write a short story suggested by one or more of the images in Text 2 (see p. 39). **(LC 2005)**

6 'The grandeur of work.' Write a speech (serious or light-hearted) in which you address your classmates or peer group on the importance of work in our lives. **(LC 2004)**

7 'In all travelling it's usually best to go along with wherever the wind blows you.' Write an article for a magazine for young adult readers in which you give advice to people intending to travel abroad for work or holiday. **(LC 2003)**

Key Points

- Remember to **plan**, **write**, **check**.

- You can plan by **brainstorming** or by making a **mind-map/diagram**.

- Each composition should have an **introduction**, **body** and **conclusion**.

- Try to get your reader's attention in the **introduction**.

- Remember to **connect each paragraph to the next** in the body of the composition.

- Don't let your essay just fizzle out – your **conclusion** should be effective.

- Always **check** your work.

- Use **comprehension texts** as a resource in the exam.

- Underline **key words** in the examination question.

- The **personal essay** offers scope for a variety of responses, e.g. narrative, argumentative.

- Other instructions may be more prescriptive.

- No length is specified, but the norm is three to five A4 pages.

- Allow approximately 20 minutes for reading, choosing questions and checking your work in Paper I.

- Allow approximately **80 minutes** for **Section II: Composing**.

- **Total marks** for composition question: **100**.

5: The Single Text

●●● Learning Objectives

In this chapter you will learn:

- How to revise the single text.

- How to answer examination questions on the single text.

Revising your chosen text

The Leaving Cert requires that you study a single text in depth and be prepared to answer questions on a variety of aspects. The headings below indicate the aspects that are relevant to any study of a **novel** or **drama**.

You can test your knowledge of your chosen text by answering the following questions.

The novel

Stages of the plot

Exposition (opening chapters):

- What is the setting and background?

- How are the characters introduced?

- How is the plot set in motion?

Complications:

- How do problems/conflicts develop?

- Do the characters and/or events precipitate the crisis?

- What outside forces are involved, if any?

- Are complications expected or surprising?

Climax/crisis:

- Is there one major crisis only, or a series of crises?

- Is tension between the protagonist (chief character) and antagonist (opposing character) brought to a head? If it is, how does this happen?

- Is the struggle internal (within the character's mind)?

- Is there actual physical danger and suspense?

Resolution:

- Predictable or surprising?

- Happy or sad?

- Open or closed, i.e. are all loose ends tied, or is there a sense that the situation is not fully resolved?

Characters and characterisation

Main characters:

- Description of appearance?

- Personality, and how is it revealed?

- Do names have any significance?

- How do they deal with problems/react to crises?

- Relationships with other characters in novel?

- Do they change/develop as people?

- Do they learn from their experiences?

- Are they influenced by setting (time and/or place)?

Setting

- Any particular context, e.g. family, village?

- Time period: present, past, future?

- Rural or urban? Is this significant?

- Does the setting have any bearing on what takes place, or is it incidental to the action/characters?

- Is social background/setting a factor?

- Are there detailed descriptions of setting? Is this significant?

Themes/issues

- Are there any clues given in the title?

- What are the characters most concerned about?

- Are there any general lessons about life to be learned from reading the novel?

- Does the writer use imagery/symbolism that might suggest themes?

Techniques of novel

- How is the story told – first person, third person, etc.?

- Is the story told in chronological order or are there flashbacks?

- Does the writer make use of parallelism/contrast/irony/foreshadowing?

- Does dialogue play a major part?

- Is the action fast paced or leisurely?

- Is there a reflective, sombre atmosphere or a dramatic, suspenseful one?

- Is imagery/symbolism central to the novel?

Your own response

- What do you especially like or dislike about the story?

- Which character do you identify or empathise with? Can you say why?

- What aspects of the novel do you find most interesting?

- What impression did the novel make on you?

- Would you recommend the novel to other readers, and why or why not?

- How did you respond to the world of the novel?

- How did you respond to the way the story was told?

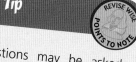

Top Tip

Questions may be asked about any one of these aspects of the novel, so know your text well.

Elements of drama

The plot

Exposition:

- Where and when is the action taking place?

- What is our first impression of the main characters? How do they reveal themselves?

- What problems/conflicts become apparent?

- What do we learn about the world of the play?

Complications:

- How do problems/conflicts develop?

- Are these complications/tensions potentially destructive, as in a tragedy, or potentially amusing, as in a comedy?

- Have they arisen because of the personality or actions of the main character?

- Have they been caused by outside influences?

- Have they arisen from relationships between the characters?

Crisis/climax:

- Is the crisis manifested in a physical way, e.g. by a battle, confrontation?

- Is the crisis manifested in the internal struggle of the protagonist (the chief character)?

- How does the dialogue indicate that a moment of great intensity has been reached?

Resolution:

- Is the play resolved in a catastrophe, i.e. involving the death of the protagonist and/or other main characters (as in a tragedy)?

- Is the ending a happy one for the leading characters, as in a comedy?

Characters/characterisation

- How do the main characters reveal themselves and their concerns?
- How do they relate to the other characters?
- What is their dramatic or symbolic function in the play?

Themes

- What issues are raised by the play – political, social, moral?
- What does the play tell us about human behaviour?
- How does the language of the play convey the dramatist's concerns?

Language and imagery

- How important are the language and imagery of the play in conveying character, theme, atmosphere?
- Is there a pattern of imagery that can be traced through the play? What is its significance?

Your own response

- How did you respond to the main character and his/her concerns?
- Which minor characters were you most in sympathy with?
- What are your impressions of the world of the play?
- Which scene(s) did you find most compelling?

Staging/performance

If you have seen a performance of your chosen play, you are free to support the points you make by reference to the performance. You should take note of the following:

- How did the **set, lighting, costumes** contribute to the atmosphere/ convey the themes of the play?
- Which aspects of the play did the director choose to emphasise?
- How did the actors interpret their roles?

Top Tip

REVISE WISE
POINTS TO NOTE

Questions may be asked about any one of these aspects of a drama, so know your text well.

- Did their interpretation correspond with your view of the characters? If not, why not?

- What was your overall response to the performance?

Writing an essay on the Single Text

First, look closely at the question and identify any key words to see what particular aspect it requires you to write about. Underline the key words.

1. Planning: Making a plan will help you to organise your answer. (See pp. 60–61 for suggestions on planning.)

2. Writing:

- Unlike your answer in the Composing section, your opening sentence does not need to be eye-catching or original. It is acceptable to **rephrase the question**, then **state clearly whether you agree, disagree or partly agree with the statement.**

- **Develop your argument**, point by point, paragraph by paragraph. Make use of **thesis or topic sentences** to direct attention to your main point.

- **Use evidence from the text** that illuminates your argument. Each paragraph should contribute to the persuasive effect of your essay.

- **Brief quotations** are more effective than long ones.

- **Try to make five to six points**, if possible.

- Your concluding paragraph should pull together your main ideas and concisely summarise how your essay has successfully answered the question.

Top Tip

Remember the three parts of any writing assignment: **planning, writing, checking**.

3. Checking: Always read over your work. You will spot at least some errors!

Sample question and answer

'The play Macbeth *has many scenes of compelling drama.' Choose one scene that you found compelling and say why you found it to be so. Support your answer by reference to the text. (LC 2004)*

I agree that *Macbeth* has many scenes of compelling drama. From start to finish the audience is involved in the dilemma of this potentially good man who, through ruthless ambition, gets caught up in a web of evil and deceit. But I would select Act II, scene ii as a particularly compelling and dramatic scene, as it encapsulates many of the concerns of the play.

The scene makes a compelling **visual impact**. It takes place at night, immediately after the murder of Duncan, which has occurred offstage. Macbeth enters, carrying the blood-stained knives which he has used to kill the king. From the beginning of the scene, Shakespeare makes us aware of the images of blood and darkness that permeate the play and give it its atmosphere of evil and violence. Images of the owl that 'screams' and the strange mutterings that Macbeth hears add to the **atmosphere of suspense**.

The scene is dramatically compelling, too, **in what it reveals to us about the characters of Macbeth and his wife**. Macbeth's rambling speech shows how close to the edge he is. He seems almost baffled by his actions as he wonders why he could not join in the prayers he overheard: 'But wherefore could not I pronounce "Amen"?' In contrast, Lady Macbeth appears to be calm and in control: 'These deeds must not be thought of/After these ways.' This suggests a growing **conflict**

between these two, hitherto united partners in crime. Our awareness of the great gulf between them grows as we hear how obsessed Macbeth is with the idea that he will never sleep again. 'Macbeth does murder sleep,' he says, a strange preoccupation in view of the fact that he has just murdered the king. Lady Macbeth is so far removed from such concerns that she says, 'What do you mean?'

But the audience soon realises that Macbeth's deed has indeed 'murdered' all the natural comforts of a human being. Never again will he enjoy the honour and respect that he earned as Duncan's loyal thane. His moral downfall has begun, as the rest of the play shows. As this scene concentrates on Macbeth's reaction to the murder, rather than the murder itself, **it enlightens us as to his inner psychological state**.

However, the reactions of both characters prove deceptive, which gives the scene great **dramatic irony**. Macbeth has just begun on his career of destruction. As we shall see, he becomes more calculating as he plots the murder of his friend Banquo and later of Macduff. We see how the 'conscience' he appears to have in Act II, scene ii disappears, although he never loses awareness of what has happened to him. In contrast, Lady Macbeth's apparent control later deserts her as she struggles to grapple with the growing distance between herself and her husband and her own conscience, as shown by her psychological breakdown in the sleep-walking scene. The conflict hinted at here foreshadows later tragic events.

As the scene progresses, the **suspense that makes it so compelling increases**. Macbeth expresses his fear and revulsion at what he has done, seeing the blood on his hands turning the 'multitudinous seas incarnadine'. His wife, terrified of discovery, is forced to return to Duncan's chamber to 'gild the faces of the grooms' with Duncan's blood. Meanwhile, there is a mysterious knocking to be heard at the castle gate, a masterly stroke by Shakespeare that adds to the suspense.

For these reasons – the horrific imagery, the suspense, the conflict, the dramatic irony, the insight into the characters – this scene seems to me to be one of the most compelling scenes in *Macbeth*.

Examination section

- The first requirement is that you know the text well (see above).

- Read the question carefully and underline the key words.

- Candidates must answer **one** question from Section I, the Single Text, from a choice of two.

- You will be invited to respond to a specific statement about the text. You must answer the question you have been set and no other. One of the greatest faults in an essay of this type is **irrelevance**.

- Another major fault is **telling the story**. You may need to narrate a brief episode/scene from the text, but always keep in mind the question: **What point am I making?** Remember, the language genre of essays like this is predominantly the **language of argument**.

- It follows that the **register (language, tone)** in which you write should be fairly formal (but not pompous!). Avoid using slang or colloquialisms.

- Select relevant evidence from the text to support and justify your own viewpoint.

- If the question contains two components, e.g. 'The play *King Lear* offers us characters who represent the *very worst* and the *very best* in human nature', be careful to answer both, as marks will be allotted accordingly. However, it may not be necessary to give exactly equal treatment to each component.

Total marks for Single Text	Time suggested
60	55–60 minutes

Practice Questions

1. 'What fascinates the reader of *Pride and Prejudice* is the relationship between the central characters of Elizabeth and Mr Darcy.' Write a response to this statement, supporting your views by reference to the text. **(LC 2006)**

2. 'The novel *Wuthering Heights* portrays a clash between two worlds represented by Wuthering Heights and Thrushcross Grange.' Discuss this view of the novel, supporting your answer by reference to the text. **(LC 2005)**

3 'Shakespeare's *Macbeth* invites us to look into the world of a man driven by ruthless ambition and tortured by regret.' Write a response to this view of the play *Macbeth*, supporting the points you make by reference to the text. **(LC 2004)**

4 '*Death of a Salesman* is a tragedy about an ordinary man in an unforgiving world.' What is your opinion of this assessment of the play? Support your answer by reference to the play. **(LC 2003)**

5 'Othello is essentially a noble character, flawed by insecurity and a nature that is naïve and unsophisticated.' Discuss this view, supporting your answer by reference to or quotation from the play.

Key Points

- Make sure you can write about the **themes**, **characters** and **techniques** of your chosen text.
- **Plan, write and check** your work, in that order.
- Use **formal language** rather than casual.
- The **language of argument** is the most useful for answering questions on the Single Text.
- Remember to develop your points in **paragraphs**.
- Allow **55–60 minutes** for this question.
- **Total marks** for Single Text: **60**.

6: The Comparative Study

In this chapter you will learn:

- How to revise for the Comparative Study.

- How to answer questions in the exam.

Introduction

In the **Comparative Study (Section II, Paper 2)**, you are asked to compare three texts, one of which may be a film, under the following headings (known as 'modes of comparison'):

- Theme or issue.

- Cultural context.

- General vision/viewpoint.

- Literary genre.

> **Top Tip**
>
> REVISE WISE POINTS TO NOTE
>
> Three of these modes will be prescribed in any given year. Only two will appear on the examination paper. Make sure you know exactly which modes are relevant for the year you are sitting the examination.

Comparing texts

- You are not required to know each of the three texts on your Comparative Study course in the same depth as your Single Text.

- Your main task is to show the examiner that you have engaged with the texts and thought about them.

- You may be invited to focus on a **key moment** from each text that illustrates the particular point you are making.

- Do not take the word 'moment' too literally here! Choose an episode, chapter, scene or film sequence that will give you enough scope to write about.

- Even if the question does not directly ask you to use key moments as a basis for your answer, it can be a useful method of organising your answer.

- Select quotations and/or references from key moments that you can use to support your discussion.

- **Always provide the context for your key moment**, e.g. 'A key moment in the film *My Left Foot* is when Christy Brown, surrounded by his family in the kitchen, first succeeds in writing the letter A with his left foot.'

> **To compare** involves finding both **similarities** and **differences** between the texts.
>
> Words used in indicating similarities include *similarly, also, likewise, in the same way, in the same manner, just as.*
>
> Words suggesting differences include *but, nevertheless, in contrast, however, on the contrary, conversely, yet.*

Comparative mode 1: Theme or issue

- A **theme** is a unifying idea or central concern developed in a text.

- An **issue** is a topic of interest or controversy that is consistently treated throughout a text.

You will have concentrated on a particular theme common to your chosen texts. Questions to ask yourself in your revision of this theme include:

- How is the theme conveyed to the reader/audience?

- How does the theme or issue apply to the characters and their relationships?

- How does the setting/atmosphere of the text relate to the theme?

- How is the theme developed in each of the texts?

- What attitude to the theme is expressed in the text – hope/despair, amusement/sorrow, indifference/cynicism?

- Is the writer/director's attitude similar to that of the characters, or does it contrast with it, e.g. does the text satirise its theme in any way?

Once you are familiar with how the theme is expressed in each of your texts, you are ready to **compare**.

Example: Theme or issue

Note: As the list of texts for comparative study is so wide, you are unlikely to have studied the particular texts discussed in the following paragraphs. They are intended merely as illustration, and do not represent completed answers.

Theme: Love and marriage

Love and marriage are central themes in Jane Austen's novel *Pride and Prejudice*, Michael Radford's film *Il Postino* and Oscar Wilde's play *The Importance of Being Earnest*.

Each of these texts treats love and marriage as an important aspect of our lives. In *Pride and Prejudice*, the Bennet family are all, in their separate ways, concerned with the issue. Mr and Mrs Bennet have five daughters who they would like to see settled in marriage. Jane Bennet falls in love quite early on in the novel. Elizabeth, from whose viewpoint we see much of the action, is at first detached from the idea of love, and then overwhelmed by it, while the younger sister, Lydia, infatuated with a young man, Wickham, elopes with him.

Similarly, the theme of love is seen as significant in the life of Mario in Radford's film, *Il Postino*. Mario, a young postman living what seems to be an uneventful life on a small Italian island, is highly impressed with the love poems of his hero, the poet Pablo Neruda. Under Neruda's influence, he develops his own skill as a romantic poet, enabling him to win the love of a beautiful young girl, Beatrice, with his **metaphors** of love. Love is the driving force in his life.

Likewise, the characters in *The Importance of Being Earnest* think and talk of love and marriage constantly. From the beginning, Jack talks of being in love with Gwendolen, the cousin of his friend Algernon. His main concern is to please Gwendolen's mother, Lady Bracknell, sufficiently in order to marry her. As the play progresses, Algernon also falls in love with Jack's ward, Cecily, and from that moment on the plot revolves around the obstacles that lie in the way of a happy ending for both couples.

However, notwithstanding the importance of love and marriage in the lives of the main characters, each of the three texts has very different attitudes to what love and marriage actually entail. *Pride and Prejudice* looks at love and marriage in a dispassionate way. It is seen as

Comment

- Words indicating comparison are highlighted in bold.

- The first point deals with similarities between the texts, e.g. the importance of love as a theme, while the second deals with differences.

- Each observation you make must be related to all three texts.

primarily an arrangement, almost like a business transaction. The famous opening line of the novel firmly establishes the connection between marriage and money: 'It is a truth universally acknowledged that a single man in possession of a large fortune must be in want of a wife.' Each of the eligible young men is described in terms of his financial worth – Mr Bingley has five thousand a year, while Darcy, the romantic hero, has ten.

On the other hand, love in *Il Postino* is associated with poetry and beauty rather than money. Mario is impressed by the relationship of Pablo Neruda and his wife as he sees them dancing and laughing together. He links it to Neruda's poetry. He, too, wants a romantic relationship in which he can praise Beatrice in his poems. Although Mario's job is not well paid, at no stage do the young lovers see their lack of money as an obstacle to their happiness.

In *The Importance of Being Earnest*, **as in** *Pride and Prejudice*, money plays an important role in romantic considerations, as we see in Lady Bracknell's famous inquisition of Jack as a prospective son-in-law in the first scene. These characters are all part of high society, where affluence is taken for granted. **But** despite this, in some ways the carefree attitude of the young people has a lot more in common with that of Mario in *Il Postino* than those of the Bennet family in *Pride and Prejudice*. (etc.)

Comparative mode 2: Cultural context

In comparing the **cultural context** of texts, you should take into account some of the following aspects:

- The **time and place** in which the text is set, i.e. the world of the text.

- The kind of **society or environment** depicted in the text – rural, urban, isolated, etc.

- The **values expressed** in that society, either openly or implicitly.

- The relative **position of men, women and children** in the world of the text.

- Attitudes to **love, marriage, power and money** almost always have a cultural context.

- Questions of **religion, work, class differences**.

Example: Cultural context

George Eliot's novel *Silas Marner*, Peter Weir's film *Witness* and Sean O'Casey's play *Juno and the Paycock* are each set in different times and places: nineteenth-century England, modern-day America and Ireland in the early twentieth century, respectively. Although the cultural contexts vary widely, there are many interesting similarities to be seen between the three texts.

Raveloe, the village in which Silas Marner lives, is a close-knit community of shared values. Religion has an unobtrusive but crucial place in the lives of the villagers. For them, Christianity is a practical faith. It involves support for one's neighbours, particularly in times of trouble. Going to church is seen as being 'neighbourly' – theological questions are of no importance. When Dolly Winthrop tries to invite Silas to come to church, it is because it is a 'good thing'; she is unable to give any conscious reasons why.

In the Amish community where much of the action in *Witness* takes place, religion involves practical help, **as in Silas Marner**. One example of this is the communal building of the barn. **Similarly**, the Amish faith entails bearing witness to goodness, and an attempt to live life in a righteous way. **Unlike** the villagers in the novel, however, for whom religion is an intuitive thing, the Amish attitude is conscious, based on strict theological rules. Dress, family structures, attitudes to work and violence are all influenced by it.

Juno and the Paycock offers us **yet another** view of religion. For Juno Boyle, the long-suffering heroine of the play, religion is a source of consolation in times of trouble, such as when her son Johnny is killed or her daughter Mary becomes pregnant out of wedlock. Here we see her simple faith in the goodness of God. Catholicism for her gives some meaning to otherwise senseless suffering. Her neighbour, Mrs Madigan, shares in her simple faith in a personal God and his mother who watches over them all. There are frequent religious references and

even prayers. **But in contrast with the other two texts**, there is no sense in the play that religion has any connection with how people behave. The behaviour of Captain Boyle and Joxer is reckless, and finally, in the case of Captain Boyle, deeply unchristian as he rejects his pregnant, unmarried daughter.

Another aspect of the cultural context of these texts is the attitude to women they express. **In each text** women play an ostensibly inferior role. Nancy, who marries the upper-class Godfrey Cass in *Silas Marner*, sees her role in passive terms. It is Godfrey who makes all crucial decisions in their marriage – who, in fact, determines even the mood of their relationship at any given time. **Similarly**, in *Witness* Rachael's roles as mother and daughter always take precedence over herself as an individual. **Likewise**, Juno Boyle's impatience with her work-shy husband belies her acceptance of her role as wife and mother. **Yet conversely**, in each text there is an underlying awareness of the power of these women within their own environment. (etc.)

Comparative mode 3: General vision and viewpoint

When comparing the general vision and viewpoint of different texts, look at the following aspects:

- What aspects of life do the texts concentrate on and why?

- What attitudes to human nature/human relationships are expressed in the texts?

- Is the 'general vision' optimistic (as in a romantic comedy) or pessimistic (as in a tragedy)?

- Is the attitude to life cynical, realistic, romantic, idealised, etc.?

- Is the viewpoint consistent throughout the text or does it change, e.g. through the use of different narrators?

- How did you respond to the general vision and viewpoint of the text?

In considering the general vision and viewpoint, remember that it is inherent within the elements of the text itself, and not imposed from any external source. Take the following into account:

- How the development of the narrative conveys the general vision and viewpoint.

- How the characters express a particular attitude to life in their actions, dialogue and relationships with others.

- How images or symbols contribute to our awareness of this viewpoint.

- In film, how the *mise-en-scène* (see p. 97) contributes to the general vision or viewpoint.

- The **ending** of a text is clearly important – does it end happily or unhappily? On a note of uncertainty, perhaps?

Example: General vision and viewpoint

The general outlook and vision of George Eliot's novel *Silas Marner*, Arthur Miller's play *Death of a Salesman* and Peter Weir's film *Witness* have some similarities as well as major differences.

Each of the texts sees the problematic nature of human experience. Silas Marner is confronted with the betrayal of his friends and the subsequent loss of his religious faith. He experiences misery and isolation in his self-imposed exile in the village of Raveloe. **Likewise**, John Book, the police officer in *Witness*, suffers the disillusionment of betrayal as he comes to realise how corrupt Schaeffer, the Chief of Police, really is. **Like Silas**, although for very different reasons, he is forced to leave his home, Philadelphia, to seek refuge with the Amish community in Pennsylvania. In *Death of a Salesman*, Willy Loman **also** has a sense of betrayal, as he realises that the career to which he has given his life has come to nothing. Society no longer needs his services. **Unlike** Silas or Book, his solution does not take the form of physical exile. **Rather**, he becomes isolated mentally and emotionally from those around him.

Each of the texts, therefore, could be said to have a pessimistic view of human nature. **Each of the characters** must undergo further suffering – Silas at the loss of his beloved gold, which had replaced human relationships in his affections; Book as he tries to escape the revenge of his former colleague; and Willy as he experiences, in flashback form, the many slights and failures that have made his life a failure.

Comment

- Words indicating comparison are highlighted in bold.

- Keep the terms of the question in mind at all times, e.g. the general vision and viewpoint.

- Relate each of your points to each of the texts.

For a time, this bleak vision seems to predominate in **all** of the texts. Silas's life in Lantern Yard paints a depressing picture of a bigoted society. Even in Raveloe, life is brutal and short for some people, such as Eppie's mother, Molly. Bad people exist here, too, such as Dunsey Cass. There is prejudice and class division. **Similarly**, Philadelphia is presented as a violent, dangerous place, even for an innocent little boy who has simply witnessed a murder. **And** in *Death of a Salesman*, twentieth-century America seems a cold, harsh place for a man who has outlived his economic usefulness.

However, this pessimism is alleviated somewhat as each of them find some refuge in the love of another human being. Silas's loneliness is overcome by the love of his adopted daughter, Eppie. Book falls in love with the Amish woman, Rachael. Towards the end of the play, Willy realises that his family loves him, despite his failings.

In **both** *Silas Marner* and *Witness*, the role of the community is crucial in helping both Silas and John Book to recover some of their faith in human nature. Raveloe, as its name suggests, is a village where human beings support each other. Religion here is seen in the form of community support. **Likewise**, the Amish community shows the value of communal help and solidarity, even to the extent of overcoming evil and danger. **But** unfortunately for Willy Loman, no such awareness of communal support exists. **Rather**, it seems as if his alienation increases, suggesting Miller's view of the fragmentary nature of modern living. Such a view is **at variance with** the **more benign** vision presented by the other two texts. (etc.)

Comparative mode 4: Literary genre

'Genre' is the term used for a type or class of composition. A literary genre is a recognisable and established category of written or cinematic work with its own conventions. In short, questions of genre revolve around the basic question: **How is the story told?**

When comparing texts under the heading of literary genre, you might take the following into account:

- Is the story told in **prose, e.g. a novel, short story**? If it is, then take into account the **main elements of fiction**:

  ❖ Narrative voice: First or third person.

- ❖ Plot/sub-plot.
- ❖ Characterisation.
- ❖ Setting/atmosphere.
- ❖ Theme.
- ❖ Style of writing: Language techniques, etc.

- Is it told as a **drama or film**? If so, take into account the **main elements of drama**:
  - ❖ Plot/sub-plot.
  - ❖ Characterisation as revealed through action.
  - ❖ Dialogue.
  - ❖ Theme.

- Also consider how **drama offers a different perspective from prose texts**, such as:
  - ❖ Presentation of conflict.
  - ❖ Performance on stage.
  - ❖ Theatrical effects.

- **Film** is a **visual medium** that shares some of the elements of fiction and drama mentioned above, e.g. **narrative, characterisation, setting, dramatic conflict, dialogue**.

- However, film has another essential element that drama lacks: the use of a **camera** to control what the audience sees.

- This is known as the ***mise-en-scène*** (literally, 'what has been put in the picture'). It includes:
  - ❖ Camera positioning and movement.
  - ❖ Lighting.
  - ❖ Sets, props, costumes, make-up.
  - ❖ Sound, including music.
  - ❖ Special effects.
  - ❖ Actors' performance.

- These aspects of a film help to create its meaning, just as a prose writer will make use of words.

Example: Literary genre

George Eliot's novel *Silas Marner*, Arthur Miller's tragedy *Death of a Salesman* and Peter Weir's film *Witness* tell the story of their hero's experience of disillusionment within the framework of different literary genres.

Each of the texts is driven by the credibility of its main character in his conflict with himself and with his society. In the novel, George Eliot builds up our sense of Silas's character by direct verbal description. As the omniscient (all-knowing) narrator, writing in the third person, she gives us an insight into the sort of person Silas becomes. Naïve and trusting at the beginning of the novel, with an inadequate understanding of human nature, it is psychologically credible that Silas should isolate himself from others at the first experience of betrayal. The plot involves his removal to a hitherto unknown place, Raveloe, where his journey into understanding begins.

Likewise, in *Death of a Salesman*, we are given an insight into an equally tormented character, Willy Loman. **But** as a drama, the conflicts between Willy's view of himself and the reality are presented **more directly** to the audience: a drama shows rather than tells its story, as a novel does. Willy reveals his character by what he says and does and how others in the drama react to him. In his exchanges with his wife, Linda, and his sons, Biff and Happy, he gives us an insight into his problems. **Unlike** the novel, there is no direct authorial comment.

Similarly, in *Witness*, dialogue plays an important part in revealing the character of John Book. **However**, in the film, other effects are equally important in building up a sense of character. Harrison Ford, the actor, brings a sense of authority to his role that gives credibility to his role as law enforcer. Facial expressions, hand gestures and body movements allow him to express emotion immediately to the audience, **unlike** the slower method employed in *Silas Marner*. Indeed, the *mise-en-scène* contributes greatly to our interpretation of Book as a character. The character's costumes, such as the conventional suit, contribute to our sense that this is a man who takes his job seriously – who plays by the book, as it were. The camera shots include frequent close-ups that allow Book to dominate the frame, which is another device of characterisation that is **unique** to film as a genre.

In *Silas Marner* Eliot makes use of imagery and symbol in characterisation. Silas's growing pile of gold, hard and sterile, becomes transformed into Eppie's golden curls, the source of his redemption. The parallel is developed in a series of poetic images. In *Death of a Salesman*, **however**, image and symbol are replaced by a number of theatrical devices that add to our sense of Willy as a complex character. These theatrical effects allow the dramatist to juxtapose characters and scenes from Willy's past with those of his present and allow Willy to comment on them. This highly stylised device **contrasts with** the more reflective and time-consuming development of character in the successive chapters in *Silas Marner*.

But film has a **corresponding device** created by the editing process, where scenes can be juxtaposed on the screen in rapid succession. We see this effect at work in the moment where Book realises the extent of Schaeffer's involvement with crime. **Like drama**, and **in contrast with** the novel, film has a limited time to tell a story, so editing techniques can speed up or slow down a scene as the director decides. *Witness*, therefore, moves **far more** rapidly from scene to scene, location to location, than *Death of a Salesman* does. (etc.)

Examination section

- Two of the three prescribed modes of comparison will appear on the paper.

- You will be required to choose **one** question, A or B.

- A choice will be offered within each question.

- The question may be allotted a global mark (70) or divided in two, 40 + 30.

- Read the questions carefully, as they can vary.

- Do **not** use the same text you have used for the Single Text question in this section.

- If you have studied Shakespeare as part of your comparative study, be careful to include it in your answer, especially if the question asks you to choose **at least two texts. (Note: Candidates at Higher Level lose marks if they omit Shakespeare.)**

- Remember to **plan, write** and **check.**

Total marks for Comparative Study	Time suggested
70	65 minutes

Practice Questions

1 Theme or issue

'The dramatic presentation of a theme or issue can add greatly to the impact of narrative texts.' Write an essay comparing how the presentation of a theme or issue, common to the texts you have studied for your comparative course, added to the impact of the texts. **(LC 2006)**

2 Cultural context

'Understanding the cultural context of a text adds to our enjoyment of a good narrative.'

In light of the above statement write an essay comparing the cultural contexts of the texts you have studied in your comparative course. Support the comparisons you make by reference to the texts. **(LC 2006)**

Key Points

- **Comparison** of texts is more important than highly detailed knowledge.

- Be familiar with modes of comparison prescribed for the year of your exam: **theme/issue**, **cultural context**, **general vision and viewpoint** or **literary genre**.

- Comparison involves **similarities** and **contrasts**.

- Relate the points you make to **each** of the texts.

- Remember to use words indicating comparison, e.g. **like**, **unlike**.

- Prepare **key moments** from texts to demonstrate the points you hope to make.

- Support your answer with relevant **quotation/ reference**.

- **Suggested time for Comparative Study: 65 minutes.**

- **Total marks: 70.**

3 General vision and view-point

'Each text we read presents us with an outlook on life that may be bright or dark, or a combination of brightness and darkness.' In light of the above statement, compare the general vision and view-point in **at least two texts** you have studied in your comparative course. **(LC 2005)**

4 Write a talk to be given to Leaving Certificate students in which you explain the term 'literary genre' and show them how to compare the telling of stories in **at least two texts** from the comparative course. **(LC 2005)**

In this chapter you will learn:

● How to approach the Unseen Poem, Question A, Section III, Paper 2.

Introduction

● In this section of the exam you will be asked to read a poem you have not seen before and respond to it.

● This is essentially a reading exercise in that you will not be required to have any information about the poem that cannot be gleaned by careful reading.

● You will have an opportunity to show that you are familiar with how poems work.

● You will also have a chance to demonstrate your own response to a poem.

Points to note

In answering the question on Unseen Poetry, keep in mind the following checklist:

● **Title**: What does it suggest to you?

● **Theme**: What is the poem saying, in your opinion? (Pay particular attention to the **first and last lines** of a poem in your attempt to interpret its theme.)

● **Speaker**: The poet's own voice, or a persona?

● **Language features**:

❖ **Denotative** (means what it says, literally).

❖ **Connotative** (meaning based on implication or association).

❖ **Imagery** (word pictures).

❖ **Simile** (comparison using **like** or **as**).

- ❖ **Metaphor** (comparison without using **like** or **as**).
- ❖ **Personification** (giving human qualities to things).
- ❖ **Symbol** (anything that stands for something else).

- ● **Sound effects:**
  - ❖ **Rhyme.**
  - ❖ **Assonance** (internal vowel rhyme).
  - ❖ **Consonance** (internal consonant rhyme).
  - ❖ **Alliteration** (repetition of consonants at beginning of words).
  - ❖ **Onomatopoeia** (words that imitate the sounds they refer to).
  - ❖ **Sibilance** (repetition of *s* or soft *c* sounds).

- ● **Tone:**
  - ❖ Feelings and emotions expressed?
  - ❖ May be ironic, i.e. saying one thing but meaning another.

- ● **Form:**
  - ❖ How is the poem organised? What is the stanza pattern?
  - ❖ Relationship between different parts?

Your response to a poem is likely to be influenced by a combination of these aspects.

Example: Section III, Poetry

Question A: Unseen Poem, Leaving Cert 2003 (20 marks)

The poet Rosita Boland reflects on the tragedy of a war-torn region in our world.

Butterflies
In Bosnia, there are landmines
Decorated with butterflies
And left on the grassy pathways
Of rural villages.

The children come, quivering down
Familiar lanes and fields.
Hands outstretched, they reach triumphant
For these bright, elusive insects–
Themselves becoming wingéd in the act:
Gaudy and ephemeral.

Question A. Write a short response to the above poem, highlighting the impact it makes on you.

Sample answer

This short poem made a powerful impact on me. What struck me first was the irony between the poem's title, *Butterflies*, as well as some of the happy, peaceful images – the 'grassy pathways', the children – and the horrific situation it describes.

The first four lines set up the contrast between the landmines in war-torn Bosnia and the butterflies that, ironically, 'decorate' them. In the second stanza we see the children, innocent and happy in their 'familiar lanes and fields', attracted as they are to the beautiful butterflies, their 'hands outstretched' to grasp them. But these fragile creatures – called 'insects' now, a word with far less innocent connotations – ironically lure the children to their deaths. I found this image of violence greatly disturbing, especially the ironic use of the word 'triumphant'.

The last two lines left me feeling even more disturbed, as I think the poet intended. The word 'wingéd' links the butterflies and the children as little angels, which might give us some consolation. The link is continued in the last line. 'Gaudy and ephemeral' is a precise description of the colourful, short-lived butterflies, but it also has horrific connotations of the colours of blood as the children are blown apart, their lives cruelly shattered. In the end, the symbolism of the butterflies is fully realised.

I found the poem powerful in its indictment of the horrors of war and its effects. In my opinion it is a moving and tender memorial to the dead children of war-torn Bosnia.

Examination section

- Read the instructions carefully, as they can vary. You may be asked to answer **two** questions (10 marks each), or **one** question (20 marks). Sometimes (but **not always**) you may be offered a choice.

- Read the poem **at least twice** before you write your answer.

- Occasionally the instructions ask for a **short response**, without specifying exactly what that entails.

- The suggested answer above is approximately 250 words. Assuming an average of nine words per line, this would give approximately 27 lines of an A4 examination script.

- If the question is in two parts, each worth **10 marks**, remember to adjust the length accordingly.

- Always **check your answer**.

Total marks for Unseen Poem	Time suggested
20	15 minutes

Practice Question

Margaret Walker is an African-American poet. In this poem she celebrates the experiences of the African-Americans.

I Want To Write
I want to write
I want to write the songs of my people.
I want to hear them singing melodies in the dark.
I want to catch the last floating strains from their sob-torn throats.

I want to frame their dreams into words; their souls into notes.

I want to catch their sunshine laughter in a bowl;
fling dark hands to a darker sky
and fill them full of stars
then crush and mix such lights till they become
a mirrored pool of brilliance in the dawn.

1 Write a response to the above poem, highlighting the impact it makes on you. (20)

Or

2 (a) Write down one phrase from the poem that shows how the poet feels about her people. Say why you have chosen this phrase. (10)
   (b) Does this poem make you feel hopeful or not hopeful? Briefly explain why. (10) **(LC 2004)**

Key Points

- Questions tend to focus on aspects such as **theme**, **language** and **personal response**.

- In your answer, take the opportunity to show your experience of **how** poems are made.

- Be familiar with **key poetic terms**, as in the checklist given on pp. 101–102.

- Read the instructions carefully, as they can vary.

- Allow **15 minutes** to answer the Unseen Poem question.

- Question is worth **20 marks**.

8: Prescribed Poetry

●●●Learning Objectives

In this chapter you will learn:

● How to answer questions on Prescribed Poetry, Question B, Section III, Paper 2.

Typical questions

Questions in this section may be phrased in different ways. For example:

● Why read the poetry of Poet A?

● Poet B: A personal response.

● Imagine you were asked to select one or more of Poet C's poems from your course for inclusion in a short anthology. Give reasons for your choice.

● Write the text of a short talk on the poetry of Poet D.

● What impact did the poetry of Poet E have on you as a reader?

You can see from the above that the questions are phrased in a user-friendly way, but they are all essentially looking for the same thing: evidence that you have engaged fully with the work of the poet under discussion.

Answering the question

If your answer is to avoid a series of vague impressions, it should show that you have **information** to give about the poet's work and that you can **make a case** for your opinions about it.

It is clear, therefore, that your experience of using the **language of information** and the **language of argument/persuasion** will be relevant in this section of the exam.

Make sure you are informed about the following aspects of a poet's work: themes; the poet's life, personality or outlook; the poet's use of language; the sounds of poetry; and poetry and the emotions.

Themes

Your answer should show that you have considered the poet's choice of themes carefully. You should illustrate your answer with examples, but make sure you don't just give a list!

Aspects of a poet's themes to consider when forming your own response include:

● Do the themes appeal to you because they reflect some of your personal concerns and interests?

● Do the themes offer an insight into the life and times of the poet?

● Do the themes enrich your understanding of universal human concerns, e.g. love or death?

● Do you respond to the themes because they are unusual or unfamiliar?

● Do you respond to themes that appeal to the intellect as well as the emotions, such as politics, religion or history?

Bear in mind that themes may be complex and open to more than one interpretation. In fact, this is often the aspect that readers respond to most.

When writing about the poet's themes, you should consider how the poet develops them in his or her work, what questions are raised in your mind and how these questions are or are not resolved.

Top Tip

Constantly ask yourself: 'What point am I making here?'

Note: Candidates in Higher Level English are penalised if they merely summarise poems.

The poet's life, personality or outlook

● Since poems are usually written out of a poet's inner emotions, concerns and conflicts, they can reveal a great deal about the personality of the poet.

● Can you build up a profile of the poet from what he or she has written, from his or her own personal voice?

- Does the poet succeed in relating personal concerns to more universal experience?

- How do you respond to the poet's voice – is it honest, convincing? Does it suggest an original or perceptive view of the world?

- Does the poet seem to you to be provocative in his or her outlook on life?

- It may be that the poet you have chosen to write about goes beyond personal revelation to create other voices, other lives. Many poets adopt a different persona to imaginatively recreate a particular experience in a particular historic context, for instance. Might this enrich our understanding of the world?

The poet's use of language

- Your response to a poet's work will be influenced by how he or she uses language. In your answer, you should include an exploration of language.

- In preparing for the examination, you should explore the **images** or **patterns of imagery** used by each of the eight poets on your course.

- When writing about imagery, try to analyse how the particular poet you are dealing with creates the effects he or she does.

- Do the images appeal to our senses? Are they effective in conveying theme or emotion?

- Are the images created by the use of **simile, metaphor, personification?**

- If the poet makes use of **symbols**, has this contributed to the poem's richness, in your view?

- Does the poet use words to **denote** (mean something literally) or to **connote** (to imply something else, or to make use of emotional associations)?

- Does the poet use poetic or conversational language, or perhaps blend the two?

- Is the language simple or complex?

The sounds of poetry

We often respond to the sounds of poetry almost before its meaning. In writing about your chosen poet, you should be able to discuss how he or she uses sound.

- Does the poet tend to use **rhyme** in a formal way, or is there a looser **sound pattern** to be heard, e.g. **alliteration, assonance, consonance**?

- Is **onomatopoeia** used?

- Is the **rhythm** of the poem fast or slow? (A detailed knowledge of metre is not necessary.)

- Your response will be much richer if it is based on close reading and attention to sound patterns and effects. Consider how the poet's use of sound patterns and effects may contribute to the theme or tone of the poem.

- It may be that the poet uses sound effects simply because of the sheer pleasure of creating musical word patterns, adding to the reader's enjoyment of the poems.

Poetry and the emotions

- The **tone** of a poem conveys the emotions that lie behind it.

- All of the elements in a poem may be used to convey tone and emotion – the poet's choice of imagery, how sound is used, the seriousness or otherwise of the theme, etc.

- Poets occasionally state their attitudes to their themes directly, but more often the approach is more subtle. Look out for the possibility of **irony**, in which the poet says one thing but clearly means something else.

- Consider what corresponding emotions are created in you as a reader of particular poems. Do you feel consoled, uplifted, provoked, disturbed, perhaps even alienated? Be confident in expressing your own response, even if it is negative.

- But bear in mind that even a heartfelt negative response must display close reading and should pay attention to specific aspects of the poems.

Top Tips

- Remember that the question will be primarily about the poetry you have studied. Do not worry unduly about the format in which the question is asked. For example, if the question asks you to write the text of a talk, it is sufficient to begin and end with the form of a talk, e.g. 'Ladies and gentlemen, today I am going to speak to you about the poetry of…Thank you for your attention.'

- As in answering questions on the Single Text and the Comparative Study, organise your answer as clearly as you can. This involves the three stages of writing: **planning**, **writing** and **checking**.

- In your plan, jot down the main points you wish to make in brainstorm or mind-map/diagram form.

- Your **introductory paragraph** should indicate the direction your answer will take.

- The **topic sentence** of each paragraph should make clear the main point you are making within the paragraph.

- Next, **develop** the point by further comment or analysis.

- Finally, **support the point by reference or quotation** from the poems.

- Follow this procedure until you have said what you have to say, then sum up in a **brief final paragraph**.

- You will be required to support your answer by reference to or quotation from the poems chosen. Long quotations are not helpful or necessary.

- It is usually better to integrate your quotations with your own sentences rather than isolating them on the page, e.g. 'Derek Mahon describes his grandfather as a harmless old man, "like a four-year old/never there when you call".'

Sample question and answer

Question: 'The appeal of Derek Mahon's poetry.'

Using the above title, write an essay outlining what you consider to be the appeal of Mahon's poetry. Support your points by reference to the poetry of Derek Mahon on your course.

Introductory paragraph indicates direction of answer.

In my view, the poetry of Derek Mahon has a tremendous appeal for contemporary readers. There are many reasons for this, among them his interesting choice of themes, his evocative use of language and his wide-ranging frame of cultural reference.

These three paragraphs deal with Mahon's concern with Irish history.

History, identity and a sense of place are among Mahon's main concerns. His own background may have contributed to his interest in such topics. Born in Belfast, later educated in Dublin, well-travelled in Europe and the United States, Mahon may be uniquely placed to look at Irish history in an objective manner. Although he rarely engages with the Northern Ireland conflict in his poems, he is always conscious of Ireland's violent past and its relationship with the present. In '**Rathlin**', the poet-visitor recalls a sixteenth-century atrocity that took place on Rathlin Island, off the coast of Antrim. Nowadays, although the place is full of a 'natural silence', being a nature reserve, it holds the memories of the horrific massacre that occurred there. The sounds heard are those of the birds rather than the 'screams of the Rathlin women'. And yet, even though this place is 'through with history', there is a sense of danger in the poet's awareness of the bombs that 'doze in the housing estates'. The last two lines reinforce this sense of insecurity about the future direction of Irish history – as he says, 'whether the future lies before us or behind'.

Old historical conflicts underlie the theme of the short lyric '**Kinsale**', but here the mood is more optimistic. The defeat of the Irish at the Battle of Kinsale in 1601 marked the end of the old Gaelic

rule. In the poem, images of brightness and hope – the yachts 'tinkling and dancing in the bay' – contrast with images of darkness and sorrow – the 'deep-delving, dark, deliberate' rain. But the future 'at last' may be hopeful for all – 'forbidden to no one'.

These themes are clearly relevant and appealing to a contemporary Irish audience, poised as we are on the brink of political change after many years of conflict. **But Mahon deals with history in a wider context also,** as seen in 'A Disused Shed in Co. Wexford'. The poem takes as its starting point the discovery of mushrooms in a disused shed. As it progresses we become aware that the mushrooms are a metaphor for the forgotten victims of all historical atrocities. Images of Peruvian mines, of the victims of the Holocaust and of genocide, and of suffering people as captured by photographs and on TV demonstrate the wide-ranging cultural references that make Mahon's poems so appealing. The mushrooms, crowding in vain towards the dim light of a keyhole, 'groaning for their deliverance', personify the patience and despair of all of these victims as they experience the nightmare of history. They are dependent on our good faith, on our acceptance of collective moral responsibility for their plight. Whereas Mahon's attitude to history has been tentative and questioning in both 'Rathlin' and 'Kinsale', in this poem he is clearly sympathetic and involved with the victims of history, as the pleading tone of the last stanza – 'save us, save us…let the god not abandon us' – suggests. Can anyone doubt the universal appeal of such a message to humanity today?

However, Mahon's interest in history extends even further, from an interest in collective experience to that of individuals in a particular social or historical context. He enters imaginatively into the mindset of these individuals in poems such as 'Ecclesiastes' and 'As It Should Be'. 'Ecclesiastes' has its roots in the Belfast of Mahon's childhood,

These paragraphs extend the main point – Mahon's treatment of the theme of history.

where Protestant preachers taught an excessively harsh version of Christianity. The speaker seems to be Mahon himself, wryly acknowledging the attraction of such attitudes: the 'fierce zeal' that nourishes the 'cold heart' and sees religion as a force for repression and gloom. Yet the poem leaves us in no doubt that this view of religion has damaged the 'credulous people' of Belfast in the past, with destructive historical repercussions. Equally fanatical are the attitudes expressed by the (possibly) Free State speaker in **'As It Should Be'**. For him, violence is justified if it achieves its aims: 'The air blows softer since his departure'. He knows no sense of doubt: 'This is as it should be'. Our knowledge of Irish history has shown us the danger of such a mindset. As these two poems show, a major appeal of Mahon's poetry is surely that his view of history is not abstract but rooted firmly in concrete situations and above all, place. Apart from the obvious titles of his poems – **'Rathlin'**, **'Kinsale'** – each of the poems I have mentioned has a distinct setting: Co. Wexford, Belfast and southern Ireland in the early twentieth century.

These three paragraphs deal with language, illustrated with quotation.

Readers of Mahon's poetry will also be attracted by his imaginative use of language, what has been called his 'acute eye and precise ear'. In **'Rathlin'** the 'natural silence' is 'slowly broken by the shearwater' – sibilance echoes the sound of the sea – and we hear the birds as they 'whistle and chatter'. Visual and aural images in **'A Disused Shed in Co. Wexford'** evoke an eerie atmosphere: the mushrooms with their 'pale flesh flaking/Into the earth that nourished it…' suggest both their actual reality and their symbolic significance as the forgotten dead. Mahon's metaphors add to the symbolism: they are 'magi, moonmen,/Powdery prisoners of the old regime', strange comparisons that evoke their mysteriousness as well as their historical resonances. He also makes use of personification ('they seem to say') and onomatopoeia (the 'cracking lock/and creak of hinges') to create an extraordinarily vivid vision in the poem. We cannot fail to be moved by the image of the mushrooms as they 'lift frail heads in gravity and good faith'.

The language of 'Kinsale' is rich in connotations, too. Heavy-sounding alliteration helps to convey the 'deep-delving, dark, deliberate' rain of the past, clearly suggesting sorrow and defeat, while sibilance ('sky-blue slates') and onomatopoeia ('tinkling') convey a sense of lightness and hope. We can appreciate why Derek Mahon has been praised for the painterly quality of his work when we read of yachts 'tinkling and dancing in the bay/like race-horses' and the 'shining windows' of the future.

Final paragraph briefly summarises main points.

Topic sentences are indicated in bold.

These aspects of his poems – the choice of relevant themes with their wide-ranging frame of cultural reference and his imaginative use of language – are in my opinion the reason why Derek Mahon's poems have an appeal for contemporary readers.

Examination section

- To date, there have been **four** questions offered in the Prescribed Poetry section.

- You must answer **one** question only.

- Prepare at least **five poets** and be very familiar with **four to five** of the six poems you have studied.

- Read each question carefully before you make your choice.

- Plan your answer.

- If the question offers you suggestions as to how you might proceed, do not ignore these suggestions – they are there to help you.

- There is no length specified, but it is reasonable to expect three to four pages to do justice to the question.

- The Department of Education and Science has published the following advice to students on answering the question on Prescribed Poetry: 'It is a matter of judgement as to which of the poems will best suit the question under discussion and candidates should not feel a necessity to refer to all of the poems they have studied.'

Total marks for Prescribed Poetry	Time suggested
50	50 minutes

Practice Questions

1 'The appeal of Eavan Boland's poetry.' Using the above title, write an essay outlining what you consider to be the appeal of Boland's poetry. Support your points by reference to the poetry of Eavan Boland on your course. **(LC 2005)**

2 'I like (or do not like) to read the poetry of Sylvia Plath.' Respond to this statement, referring to the poetry by Sylvia Plath on your course. **(LC 2002)**

3 Write an essay in which you outline your reasons for liking/not liking the poetry of Philip Larkin. Support your points by reference to the poetry of Larkin that you have studied. **(LC 2001)**

4 What impact did the poetry of John Montague have on you as a reader? Support your answer by reference to or quotation from the poems on your course.

5 'Why read the poetry of…?' (give the name of a poet of your choice). Support your answer by quotation or reference.

Key Points

- Be familiar with **themes** and **use of language** of the poets on your course.
- The **sounds** and **emotions** of poems are important.
- Form **your own response** based on close reading of the poems.
- **Plan, write and check** your answer.
- Support your points with **quotation** or **reference**.
- **Avoid summarising** poems.
- Spend approximately **50 minutes** on this question.
- **Total marks: 50.**

REVISE WISE
STUDY PLAN

Date

Time

Section to
be revised

Date

Time

Section to
be revised

Date

Time

Section to
be revised

Date

Time

Section to
be revised

Date

Time

Section to
be revised

Date

Time

Section to
be revised

Night before exam

Sections to
be revised

Glossary of Terms

aesthetic use of language: Language used primarily for artistic purposes.

alliteration: Repetition of consonant sound, usually at beginning of words.

anecdote: Very short story used to illustrate a point.

assonance: Repetition of identical vowel sound in words used together.

ballad: Folk song or poem that tells a story. Ballads normally have four lines in each stanza, with the second and fourth line rhyming.

blank verse: Unrhymed iambic pentameter, often used in long poems and particularly by Shakespeare.

climax/crisis: Moment of great intensity in a story, play, etc.

close-up: Photograph or film shot taken near at hand.

colloquialism: Informal or conversational language.

comparative literature: Study of the relationships, similarities and/or contrasts between different texts (including film) by different authors.

convention: Any aspect of a text which authors/audience accept as normal in that kind of text.

consonance: Repetition of consonant sounds in neighbouring words.

critical analysis: Examination and discussion of different aspects of a poem, novel, film, etc.

diction: Choice of words used in a literary work.

dramatic irony: When the audience at a play/film knows more about a character's situation than the character himself or herself knows.

emotive language: Words or phrases that cause an emotional response in the reader.

end-rhyme: Rhyme occurring at ends of lines.

exposition: Opening scenes of a story or drama.

fable: Brief tale containing a moral lesson.

fantasy: Type of literature based on imaginary rather than realistic persons or events.

first person narrative: Story told from the point of view of the first person, I.

genre: Type of text, e.g. poetry, fiction, film.

hyperbole: Exaggeration for the sake of effect.

imagery: Pictures created by words.

irony: Saying something while meaning something else.

language of argument: Language used to make a case for something.

language of information: Language used to convey information.

language of persuasion: Language used to persuade or convince.

language of narration: Language used to tell a story.

lyric: Fairly short poem expressing the personal feelings of a particular speaker.

metaphor: Comparison used without using the words 'like' or 'as'.

mood: Atmosphere or feeling of a poem or other text.

novel: An extended fictional narrative.

onomatopoeia: Words that seem to echo the sound they refer to.

persona: Speaker in a poem or play who is different from the poet or playwright.

personification: When animals or things are referred to as if they were human.

paradox: Language that expresses a truth in what seems at first to be a contradiction.

plot: Pattern of events in a story, play, etc.

protagonist: Main character in a drama.

pun: Play upon words alike in sound but different in meaning.

register: Appropriate tone or language used in different situations.

resolution: How a story or drama is concluded.

rhyme: Matching sounds, usually at ends of words.

rhythm: Beat or pace of words in poetry.

setting: Where and when a story takes place in a novel, film, etc.

simile: Comparison made using the words 'like' or 'as'.

soliloquy: Speech made by one character as he/she is alone on stage.

sonnet: Poem of 14 lines.

sound effects: Words chosen for their sounds as well as their meaning.

stanza: A section of a poem, separated by spaces when printed.

style: The way a writer writes – choice of language, expression, etc.

sub-plot: Minor storyline that takes place alongside the main plot.

symbol: Type of image in which something is used to represent something else.

target audience: The intended audience for an advertisement, etc.

theme: The main idea in a story, poem, etc.

tone: The attitude expressed by the speaker of the poem; the mood or atmosphere of a play, poem, etc.

tragedy: A serious play depicting the downfall of a central character.

villain: Principal evil character in a play or story.

voice: The speaker of the poem (not always intended to be the poet himself or herself).

Acknowledgements

For permission to reproduce copyright material, grateful acknowledgement is made to the following:

Extract from *Memoir* by John McGahern, courtesy of Faber and Faber Ltd.

Extract from *Bridget Jones's Diary* © Helen Fielding, 1996, courtesy of Gillon Aitken Associates.

The articles 'Oh, brother... where did it all begin?' by John Meagher, *Irish Independent*, 30 May 2005, and 'Hooked on crime', *Irish Independent*, 17 November 2005, courtesy of the *Irish Independent*.

Martin Luther King's Civil Rights Speech, Washington 1963. Reprinted by arrangement with the Estate of Martin Luther King Jr., c/o Writers House as agent for the proprietor, New York, NY. Copyright 1963 Martin Luther King Jr.; copyright renewed 1991 Coretta Scott King.

The advertising feature 'Come and see Ireland's wild side', courtesy of Tourism Ireland.

The article 'Irishmen a washout for cleaning, laundry and cooking' by Frank McNally, *The Irish Times*, 29 November 2005, courtesy of *The Irish Times*.

'The Family of Man', photographs by Edward Steichen, courtesy of Joanna T. Steichen.

Extracts from *Hidden Lives – A Family Memoir* by Margaret Forster and *The Grapes of Wrath* by John Steinbeck, courtesy of Penguin Books.

Extract from *Women and War* by Jenny Matthews, courtesy of Metz and Schilt. Copyright 2003/2006 Jenny Matthews, London/Mets & Schilt Publishers, Amsterdam.

The article 'We are not uniform individuals' by Elaine Lynch, courtesy of the author.

The article 'The filth and the fury' by Luíseach nic Eoin, courtesy of the author.

'His First Flight' by Liam O'Flaherty, from *The Short Stories of Liam O'Flaherty* (Re-published by Palgrave Macmillan in March 2006), reproduced with permission of Palgrave Macmillan.

The poem 'Butterfiles' by Rosita Boland, from *Dissecting the Heart* (2003), by kind permission of the author and The Gallery Press, Loughcrew, Oldcastle, County Meath, Ireland.

The poem 'I Want to Write' by Margaret Walker, courtesy of University of Georgia Press.